EARTH SONGS

Earth Songs

A Resurgence anthology of contemporary eco-poetry

Edited by Peter Abbs

Green Books

in association with

Resurgence magazine

First published in 2002
by Green Books Ltd
Foxhole, Dartington
Totnes, Devon TQ9 6EB
www.greenbooks.co.uk

in association with
Resurgence magazine
Ford House, Hartland,
Bideford, Devon EX39 6EE
www.resurgence.org

Cover design by Rick Lawrence
Cover illustration © Haku Shah

Text printed by Biddles Ltd, Guildford, Surrey
on Five Seasons 100% recycled paper

British Library Cataloguing in Publication Data
available on request

ISBN 1 903998 17 4

Contents

THE LIVING WORLD

LANDSCAPES AND INSCAPES

THE HOME OF EXPERIENCE

THE ECOLOGY OF LOVE

WEAVING THE SYMBOLIC WEB

THE SEARCH FOR ENLIGHTENMENT

For the next generation and especially for:

Imogen, Bryony and Samuel

Preface

Though an undoubted improvement on decades of destructive indifference and denial, there's something about our technocratic, economistic approach to the environment today that still conspires to 'unweave the rainbow'. No amount of sound environmental management will get us back in balance with the natural world if we remain deaf to the voice of the Earth speaking through us, blind to Nature's real power and beauty, and incapable of conversing with the life forces that sustain us. There are many different ways of opening ourselves to those deeper connections, but poetry for and about the earth — or Gaia — is for many a cornucopian source of atonement, enlightenment and joyful celebration. As you'll see from this anthology, no other environmental magazine gives such pride of place to earth poetry than *Resurgence*. This inspiring anthology offers a profound poetic representation of our age, and I recommend it wholeheartedly.

Jonathon Porritt
6th June 2002

Introduction

The earth is our home. It is where we have come from, the place where we live and have our being. We humans are extraordinary, symbol-makers and city builders, but we still belong with all the other diverse species in a complex web of connection and reciprocity. We are highly creative but, as our history shows, we are also perverse, dangerous and hugely destructive. And it would seem at the moment, mesmerized by the chimera of unending material progress, we are bent on desecrating our natural world and destroying ourselves with it.

Each day the ecological disasters sweep in, get briefly aired on chat shows and illustrated in lavish documentaries, and then get swamped in a surfeit of entertainment, drowned in a tidal wave of trivia. Is it that we do not want to hear the dark news? Do not want to connect the fate of our sick planet to our daily lives, to the next glossy advert for the latest (polluting) car or yet another shopping spree? Yet however we seek to suppress, displace or disown it, the spectre of extinction will not go away. To take global warming alone, scientists are predicting within decades extreme climactic conditions, the disappearance of coral reefs and tropical rain forests, the extinction of many species, the flooding of great historic cities, a pandemic of disease spreading around the whole alarmed biosphere. Somewhere at the back of our distracted minds we are all vaguely aware of this — but we resist taking the knowledge fully into our imagination, into our conscience, into the rhythm of our actual lives.

It is the prospect of such ecological disaster that has given birth to this anthology of poetry. For many of our best contemporary poets are giving voice to what must be the greatest issue of our time: *the continuing violation of the natural order and its catastrophic effect on all of life.* Is there a creative future for our earth and its rich heritage of biological life? Or are we racing towards the end of nature and a man-made apocalypse?

This anthology, however, is not confined to our relentless plunder of nature and the bleak future that may face us. Drawing imaginative attention to this is necessary, but radical curative action can only take place when we truly love the great diversity of nature, the beauty and mystery of the biosphere. The larger, the more encompassing, our vision of nature, the more sensitive and fitting will be our action. Thus many of the poems gathered here are moving celebrations: affirmations of the elements, of the outer and inner structures of the material world, of wildlife, of the seasons, of landscape, of wilderness, of the primordial. In the poetry there is a sense of inhabiting a natural world where the ecology of our spirit and the ecology of our love belong—for nature, in all its glorious specificity, forms the deep metaphors of our search for meaning and the images of our most creative moods and relationships.

It can be no accident that many of our best contemporary poets, defying nearly all current literary fashions—a metropolitan critic said recently that there could be no more nature poetry—are now writing an eco-poetry of such precision, power and lyrical elegance, and doing so in a variety of traditional and modern forms. Ezra Pound, using a striking ecological image, once called poets the antennae of the race. According to Pound, poets were the ones—not politicians, not journalists, not publicists—who most truly apprehend the state of affairs and anticipate most clairvoyantly the shape of things to come. Some of the poets gathered here are warning us of ecological disaster; others are inviting us to experience through the imagination the wealth of the earth so that we may cherish it, take it into our consciousness and become responsive and responsible to it. *But taken as a whole the poems are directing our attention to the state of nature and its place in our lives.* This is their theme, their burden and their song. The voices, bearing the momentous, if widely suppressed, agenda of the 21st Century, need to be heard.

In making the choice of poems I have employed five simple criteria: all the poets had to be alive, they had to be writing in the English language, they had to be concerned with the ecological in its broadest reading, their work had to possess intrinsic poetic merit; and no contributor, however good, could be represented by more than six poems.

Startled at finding so many eco-poems and, indeed, so many eco-poets I was, for a time, at a loss as how to organize the anthology. Then it became clear that the best way to shape the volume was by presenting the poems thematically so that they stood in their own right but could also be read as a collective narrative, a kind of verbal symphony. I also felt the themes would make the anthology more accessible, so that readers could quickly find what concerns most interested them. I would like to conclude by briefly indicating the scope and purpose of these eight themes.

The first theme is **Naming Gaia**. As most people know, Gaia is the classical Greek name for the earth Goddess. The title has been recently employed by ecologists to denote the homeostasis of the biosphere. This section, therefore, presents poems of cosmic import. The poems celebrate the elemental powers of the earth and our engaged relationship to them.

The second theme is **Our Sick Planet**. This section is the antithesis to the first. Instead of the beauty of the natural world, it reveals its ruthless desecration. It evokes the effects of pollution and the continuous threat to wildlife. Characteristically, one poem — a villanelle — is simply titled *Spurned Goddess*.

The third theme is **The Living World**. This is a selection of epiphanies. The poems here are loving and personal testimonies to wildlife, from grebes, curlews and hawks to moths, dragonflies and eels. This section is an evocation of all that abundant natural life which is now so much in question.

The fourth theme is **Landscapes and Inscapes**. This section turns to the power of landscape, those natural places that ineffably draw our spirit, feed our inner life, and all but define who we are.

The fifth theme is **The Home of Experience**. This section brings out the simple fact that we live in the biosphere, that it is all there for us to ponder, to explore, to relate to. Many of the poems catch the sheer all but inexpressible *thisness* and *thatness* of our experience before nature, whether it is the stars coming out or the apples sweetening in the dark or the moths fluttering at dusk. Other poems show how natural objects and living creatures can become the charged metaphors for the dramas of human life.

The sixth theme is **The Ecology of Love**. As a species our greatest achievement must, surely, be love. No ecological theory of life worthy the name can leave it out. This section concentrates on the power of love and especially *the sense of universal solidarity that invariably accompanies it*. The biologist Edward O. Wilson has recently coined the word *biophilia,* love of nature. The poems in this chapter suggest that the best route to biophilia is the route of erotic love — for erotic love connects us to all that lives and all that desires to live. This is the ecology of love.

The seventh theme is **Weaving the Symbolic Web**. This section concentrates on human creativity. We are, above all else, symbol-makers. It is our biological nature to make, to play, to symbolize. *Our habitat is culture.* We find and lose ourselves in our languages, our religions, our philosophies, our sciences, our theories, our arts and rituals. One of the biological functions of poets is to secure the collective habitat by keeping alive, however subversively, the inherited symbols and myths. The poems are all vivid examples of this vital survival mechanism.

The last theme is the **The Search for Enlightenment**. This needs little explanation. Because of the gift of consciousness, we see in a new light. So far, that light has not been brought to bear dramatically on the current state of the earth, nor has it fully connected its sick state with our short-term industrial and commercial drives. If our quest for wisdom cannot expand to include nature in all its plenitude and beauty, then it is likely that we will destroy not only ourselves but the great biosphere that has given birth to us. The poems in this closing section are out to locate, through the power of metaphor and the beat of cadence, the missing wisdom.

Finally, I must thank Julia Martin-Woodbridge for her work in preparing the script for publication. Her support has been invaluable.

Peter Abbs

Naming Gaia

When first seen from outside and
compared as a whole planet with its lifeless
partners, Mars and Venus, it was impossible to
ignore the sense that the Earth was a strange and
beautiful anomaly. These dead planets are,
visually as well as chemically, a neutral
background against which the living planet
Earth shines like a dappled sapphire.

James Lovelock

Prayer for the Great Family

Gratitude to Mother Earth, sailing through night and day—
    and to her soil: rich, rare and sweet
        in our minds so be it.

Gratitude to Plants, the sun-facing light-changing leaf
    and fine root-hairs; standing still through wind
    and rain; their dance is in the flowing spiral grain
        in our minds so be it.

Gratitude to Air, bearing the soaring Swift and the silent
    Owl at dawn. Breath of our song
    clear spirit breeze
        in our minds so be it.

Gratitude to Wild Beings, our brothers, teaching secrets,
    freedoms, and ways; who share with us their milk;
    self-complete, brave, and aware
        in our minds so be it.

Gratitude to Water: clouds, lakes, rivers, glaciers;
    holding or releasing; streaming through all
    our bodies salty seas
        in our minds so be it.

Gratitude to the Sun: blinding pulsing light through
    trunks of trees, through mists, warming caves where
    bears and snakes sleep—he who wakes us—
        in our minds so be it.

Gratitude to the Great Sky
    who holds billions of stars—and goes yet beyond that—
    beyond all powers, and thoughts
    and yet is within us —
    Grandfather Space.
    The Mind is his Wife.

        so be it.

                (after a Mohawk prayer)
                Gary Snyder

Rough Country

Give me a landscape made of obstacles,
of steep hills and jutting glacial rock,
where the low-running streams are quick to flood
the grassy fields and bottomlands.
                                A place
no engineers can master—where the roads
must twist like tendrils up the mountainside
on narrow cliffs where boulders block the way.

Where tall black trunks of lightning-scalded pine
push through the tangled woods to make a roost
for hawks and swarming crows.
                                And sharp inclines
where twisting through the thorn-thick underbrush,
scratched and exhausted, one turns suddenly

to find an unexpected waterfall,
not half a mile from the nearest road,
a spot so hard to reach that no one comes—

a hiding place, a shrine for dragon flies
and nesting jays, a sign that there is still
one piece of property that won't be owned.

Dana Gioia

Incandescence

The earth remembers in the dark
a spark that glowed before a star,
before a thought, before we were;
the time before the cosmic arc

brought from darkness into light
the urgent beast of consciousness
that walked the surface searching space
nostalgic for the velvet night

within the void and finding death
attending life, light ending dark.
With each and every indrawn breath
we co-exist with that first spark

which flared to form the face of God;
a hint of truth in all that's said.

Ted Walter

Gold Has an E-Number

A pinch emblazons exotic chocolates,
sifted fire
glitters on opulent foods.
We can eat gold.

Born in heat,
our bones and wires are part
of an architecture of sky,
like stars,
constructed from chemical meshes.

Life
must lie in the hinges,
the gaps, alchemies of exchange,
dynamic mixings.

We have power
to increase connections,
deep detritus from the universe
massed in our heads,

thoughts, ignitions;

each one of us processes
the solar system,
we add
to the recipes of moons and quarks.

Isobel Thrilling

Air: an Aria

To be air, atmosphere
To be what substantial phenomena are not
       but not insubstantial
To embrace, to enclose
To be a gaseous ocean on whose floor creatures walk
       through whose depths creatures swim
To contain even a planet in one's blue envelope

To be subtle, to be intricate
To fill interstices
To abhor vacua
To treat democratically all geometries
To caress with indifference iron flesh water
To flow, to be liquid
       but not as liquid is

To be everything's outside
To be inside also
To be sucked into lungs along with smoke and smells
To assume inner shapes, as of bagpipes, bellows,
       balloons, basketballs
To erupt from constriction in a belch or a fart
To be the stuff of inflation
       but amenable to government
To fuel filibusters, put the wind into windbags
To be needed
To be taken for granted also

To constitute a medium where things may go hang:
clouds hawks helicopters hang-gliders
       and the dust-motes
that glitter in oblique shafts of light in silent rooms

Richard Poole

Flood

Water asleep
all across China,

cool days and nights
of water sleeping

and growling
in its sleep,

young dog water,

and stars wanting
to be held tight,

and the rain lingual
as ever,

and China folding hands
idiomatically,

and water expatiating
and dreamy,

and not writing anything down,
and the rivers

in endless revolution,
winding in psycho-sensual economy

round and round
the scenic perfumeries,

the hills and other illuminants:

water asleep
as it circles China,

inundating the palaces,
unplanning the cities,

and floating the Buddhas
downstream in their sleep.

Penelope Shuttle

The Rain Forest

A green ape, drinker of clouds,
always thirsty,
always swollen with rain.

His fur matted and dripping,
his face glistening
in patches of watery sunlight;
his eyes are water moving
over gray sand,
peering and drinking.

He shrinks away as night comes,
and the red cedar of dreams
grows in his place
from yellowing roots, its bark
the colour of rust and old blood;
dead leaves cling there,
caught in crevices.
Night fills
with the shadowy life of fish
that spawn under sunken logs.

But the green ape always returns;
he stands and watches,
his broad feet clenched in a soil
through which the daylight
seeps and darkens...

Though the ape has not yet spoken,
I listen this evening
to drops of water,
as one might listen
to a tongue growing green.

John Haines

Gifts of Rain

I
Cloudburst and steady downpour now
for days,
       Still mammal,
straw-footed on the mud,
he begins to sense weather
by his skin.

A nimble snout of flood
licks over stepping stones
and goes uprooting.
             He fords
his life by sounding.
                Soundings.

II
A man wading lost fields
breaks the pane of flood:

a flower of mud-
water blooms up to his reflection

like a cut swaying
its red spoors through a basin.

His hands grub
where the spade has uncastled

sunken drills, an atlantis
he depends on. So

he is hooped to where he planted
and sky and ground

are running naturally among his arms
that grope the cropping land.

III

When rains were gathering
there would be an all-night
roaring off the ford.
Their world-schooled ear

could monitor the usual
confabulations, the race
slabbering past the gable,
the Moyola harping on

its gravel beds:
all spouts by daylight
brimmed with their own airs
and overflowed each barrel

in long tresses.
I cock my ear
at an absence—
in the shared calling of blood

arrives my need
for antediluvian lore.
Soft voices of the dead
are whispering by the shore

that I would question
(and for my children's sake)
about crops rotted, river mud
glazing the baked clay floor.

IV

The tawny guttural water
spells itself: Moyola
is its own score and consort,

bedding the locale
in the utterance,
reed music, an old chanter

breathing its mists
through vowels and history.
A swollen river,

a mating call of sound
rises to pleasure me, Dives,
hoarder of common ground.

Seamus Heaney

Lumber

Full moon, the hills are flying
Orion like a kite,
I feel the tug of silver.

Shropshire is heavy with stars,
a fossil of ancient seas,
Long Mynd encumbered with shells,
the rigging of creatures
wrecked in rock,
lost maps of wings and fins.

The planet aslant is twisting
lava-strings, red ropes
for future continents,
embryo oceans
locked in ice and atoms.

My father's bones are part
of the county now,
we come from the lumber of space,
seed of light, fissions
from suns and radiations,
souls grown in chemistries
deep in the dark matter.

The little town
is weighted with lamps,
its church fixed firm as a molar.

Isobel Thrilling

A Brief History of Light

And the light shineth in darkness;
and the darkness comprehended it not.

The dazzle of ocean was their first infatuation,
its starry net, and the fish that mirrored it.
They knew enough to know it was not theirs.
Over the hill a dozen furnaces glowed,
the gold gleamed that was smelted in secret,
and the trapped white light shone bitterly
at the heart of the hardest stone on earth.
But they knew enough to know it was not theirs.
Then their hoards of light grew minor,
since none could view the sun straightly,
and jealousy burned their lives to the core.
So they made a god of it, shedding glory,
shedding his light on all their arguments.
Did they know enough to know it was not theirs?
The god in his wisdom preceded them westwards,
and the forests, in whose pillared interiors
black shapes dwelled, were banished for good.
They promised an end to the primitive darkness:
soon there was nothing that was not known.
They thought: *Our light is made, not merely reflected —*
even the forked lightning we have braided!
And they banished the god from the light of their minds.
But they mistook the light for their knowledge of the light,
till light, and only light, was everywhere.
And they vanished in this, their last illumination,
Knowing barely enough to know it was not theirs.

Catrióne O'Reilly

Solstice

The Sun must move, if it is a fire, because Fire is the most mobile of the elements. When we prevent flames from rising, when we imprison them in the bowels of the furnace, they twist impatiently about themselves. (La Cena dei Ceneri)

Hot yellow moon rose
last night, transformed
into sun, deep gold
over intense black rustling
leaves breathing stored
green scent of long day;
so all night the sky
shone, there was no night:
the triumph of light

renewed, Summer, most fiercely
hoped-for, called up
out of strength in the cold
months, with force,
with images of lions.
Sun in glory, at
zenith, convulsed with fire;
astronomers predict
magnetic surges, solar storms,
electrical disruption, flares
leaping millions of miles.

When the transformation
comes, it will be sudden
gold forming in the crucible.

Hilary Llewellyn-Williams

Engineering

Stars:

Not set like necklaces
or brooches,
not pulsing quietly
through atmospheric velvets,
chiffons of mist,

ROARING.

If there is a music of
the spheres,
it's heavy-metal,
howling ingots of sound
ripping
textures of the firmament.

Not free-wheeling;

these behemoths of space
follow patterns
laid by laws
not invented by man;

krakens of light and dark
penned into
fireballs, cosmic clouds, pits,

fix a kind
of harvest—a leaf, a child, love.

Isobel Thrilling

Women Dancing in a Field of Poppies

(from Earth Song Cycle)

Slowly at first they measure
their steps as the sun strengthens,
the poppies flame redder,
the sea-blue deepens, and they,
women in white, loose-limbed,
flowing, circle hand in hand,
turn faster, and faster,
leap and fly till their feet
are birds, white birds, skimming.
And round they go, wing to wing,
as the field revolves and the sea,
and earth veils and unveils,
white and blue, under their heels,
which skim and pause and come to rest
while round and round them turns
the scarlet field,
       and O the earth.

Jeremy Hooker

Our Sick Planet

We did not expect the earth to be vulnerable,
capable of health or sickness, wholeness or
injury. But it turns out that we were wrong;
the earth is now unmistakably sick.

Mary Midgley

The Fish are all Sick

The fish are all sick, the great whales dead,
The villages stranded in stone on the coast,
Ornamental, like pearls on the fringe of a coat.
Sea men who knew what the ocean did,
Turned their low houses away from the surf.
But new men, who come to be rural and safe,
Add big glass views and begonia beds.

Water keeps to itself
White lip after lip
Curls to a close on the littered beach.
Something is sicker and blacker than fish.
And closing its grip, and closing its grip.

Anne Stevenson

Plenty

The phrase seemed right for the time. *There are*, we'd say,
plenty more fish in the sea. I taste it again, the heady
mixture of greed and insouciance; the future waiting
for what we might care to do to it.

                                Have I invented
these insistent images? Trawlers strung out across a pale
expanse of sea in stormlight, their brown hulls shrouded
in luminous spray; the wet ropes taut, the seethe and slide
of life plucked from the prodigal waters. Strong hands
guiding the swollen nets; the holds crammed full, the decks
shining with scales. All this
like some grained newsreel, the residual shadow of a world
we loved unwisely.

                                Where shall we go from here,
knowing what we know? Spillage and exploitation, repeated
patterns of violation; soft white bellies turning
to an impassive sky. Our children know it too, the stench
blown from the littered shoreline, the struggle for release

from stifling dreams; the ineluctable roles played out
in rented bedrooms to the scream of gulls, the wind
rattling the casements; the unemployed
haunting the sullen back-streets; the deserted quays.

Jem Poster

Seals in Berlin

They cry in the city,
their mouths the 'O's of children
starving at their mothers' skirts.

Up and down they go
in a churn of milky water,
belly-gleam in frozen light.

Turn and turn again,
breaking the water chains
at the breached wall.

Their hearts are arctic,
their small waves break
on the shores of a poisoned earth.

In each brain the North Sea,
instinct Baltic,
their small skulls ice.

Again, again.
They will not give up.
O. O. Cry fathoms.

Gillian Clarke

Spurned Goddess

Let us consider Earth, explore the ache
that comes from losing touch with where we've been.
Fifteen billion years it took to make

the Earth from star-stuff, us. And now we take:
we overfish, we tamper with the gene.
Let us consider Earth, explore the ache.

Residual pesticides, a lifeless lake.
A forest turns to ash. Remember green?
Fifteen billion years it took to make.

Forged first in cosmic fire we cannot fake
a species. Dead, it does not rise again.
Let us consider Earth, explore the ache.

Spurned goddess; will our children learn to speak
her name in hope, honour her return?
Fifteen billion years it took to make

this peopled planet. Was it a mistake?
Will we find the slate can be wiped clean?
Let us consider Earth, explore the ache.
Fifteen billion years it took to make.

Ted Walter

Elegy

This is a summer of heat but not light,
the dim gardens uninhabited at dusk
that drifts pale blue and slightly smoke-soiled,
holding little hope of one ripe star.

Only Beech House slowly electrifies,
its windows coloured screens on a light-box module.
If you turned enough dials, would marvellous rainbows flow?
No, these are simply room-lights; distant specks

move, eat and die in them.
Generations of lives, they are stockpiled here
or set in rows behind the angular porchways
of Foxcombe and Applegarth, the bulldozed woodlands.

These are the stone fields where the poor are seeded
by random bureaucratic winds.
If they fail to root, there are priests and a welfare service:
no need to cut throats, scream, jump off balconies.

But the summer breeds its own ills. Each night
smashed glass chimes the hour, and wishes bleed
down walls autographed by the nameless young,
spilling their small fire into a granite tundra.

Carol Rumens

The Storm Cloud

John Ruskin describes the weather near the end of the 19th Century.

A thousand miles square and five miles down
It blows in, blots out the sun.
I call it the plague-wind; I name it the storm-cloud.

What does it feel like? A terminus. The stop of time.
The strawberries rot on their stems —
For a month or more now not an hour of sunshine —

And the roses in the garden hang sponges of vinegar.
I'm a hunter of hieroglyphs;
In every metallic drop of rain I see a barren star

And on stormy days leaves against the open window
Tremble continuously and hiss into
Sulphur-mists. Aspens of the apocalypse! Winds blow

The belching smoke across the stricken land. I read
The age in smouldering rivulets of
Fire, black snow, low toxic clouds, lists of children dead

Or slowly dying. Tonight I see a burning child
Rise through the millennial flames,
A charred Christ who sings: *we're at the thresh-hold —*

The uncreation now begins. Half-mad, I record what I can —
Cracked conduit of visions
And blizzards: *oh blanched sun, oh withered grass, oh blinded man.*

Peter Abbs

The Objective Naturalist

after W. D. Campbell

This remnant of a once ancient forest—
Wychwood—is now a pheasant reserve.
Seventy-two year I have known it, a lifetime,
and lived twenty-one of them in its midst—
formative years. I have seen many changes,
both for better and for worse, but on balance—
even allowing for the blur of nostalgia—
the worse weigh heavier.

                        Red squirrels
have completely disappeared; rapacious greys
ensure a paucity of hazel-nuts
in copses. Where nightjars were plentiful,
on heath whose acidic sand lies upon limestone,
nights are haunted by their absent wings.
I have not seen a grass-snake for all of twelve years,
nor any of those butterflies—the dark green,
the silver-washed, the high brown fritillary—
which once fluttered here in their hundreds.
Roman snails, abundant in the past, are few.
Certain common orchids—the two kinds
of butterfly, and some helleborines—
are virtually extinct: for fallow deer,
escaping from the deer-park in wartime,
cropped their flower-spikes.

                   I comforted myself,
until this May, that in the forest-streams
crayfish were as numerous as ever.
A delusion.
Consecutive forays have uncovered not one—
though I left, of course, no stone unturned.

Richard Poole

Penitence

I was driving into the wind
on a northern road,
the redwoods swaying around me like a black ocean.
        I'd drifted off: I didn't see the deer
till it bounced away,
the back legs swinging outwards as I braked
and swerved into the tinder
of the verge.
        Soon as I stopped
the headlamps filled with moths
and something beyond the trees was tuning in,
a hard attention
boring through my flesh
to stroke the bone.
        That shudder took so long
to end, I thought the animal had slipped
beneath the wheels, and lay there
quivering.
        I left the engine running; stepped outside;
away, at the edge of the light, a body
shifted amongst the leaves
and I wanted to go, to help, to make it well,
but every step I took
pushed it away.
        Or—no; that's not the truth,
or all the truth:
now I admit my own fear held me back,
not fear of the dark, or that presence
bending the trees;
not even fear, exactly, but the dread
of touching, of colliding with that pain.
I stood there, in the river of the wind,
for minutes; then I walked back to the car
and drove away.

        I want to think that deer
survived; or, if it died,
it slipped into the blackness unawares.
But now and then I drive out to the woods
and park the car: the headlamps fill with moths;
and woods tune in; I listen to the night
and hear an echo, fading through the trees,
my own flesh in the body of the deer
still resonant, remembered through the fender.

John Burnside

Road-side Deaths

On the same day two animals on the track to the coast—

First, a red fox slumped by the steep lane's bank.
It lay with its front paws delicately crossed as if asleep,
But its jaws were clenched in a snarl and its entrails stank

On the hot tarmac. I yanked it by its back leg and dropped
It into cool shadow and scrub on the unseen slope,
Plucking what sparse leaves I could to green its matted head.

On the next stretch a badger sprawled near the road's ditch
In a swirl of metal heat and carbon monoxide.
I imagined the driver—the musak drumming at fever pitch—

Slamming the beast and speeding on. In his small inferno
What did he see but a TV blur on the car's dark screen?
What did he hear but the crass murderous crescendo

Of the disco beat? I picked up the unmourned carcass
And tossed it on the scorched grass. There are no elegies.
No rites, no burials. The glinting cars swish past.

Peter Abbs

The Earth Rising

The men who first set foot on the bleached waste
That is the moon saw rising near in space
A planetary oasis that surpassed
The homesick longings of their voyaging race:

Emerald and ultramarine through a white haze
Like a torn veil—as if no sand or dust
Or stain of spilt blood or invading rust
Corrupted it with reds, browns, yellows, greys.

So visionaries have seen it: to design
Transparent, luminous and, as if new-made,
Cut from surrounding darkness. Praise the Lord,
For *Heaven and earth* (the psalmist sang) *are thine*;
The foundation of the round world thou hast laid,
And all that therein is. And plague and sword.

                                        Clive Wilmer

Poem for the End of the World

Some day, it seems, the cosmos,
Turning impatient, will throw a planet at us,
Or else a filthy snowball of a comet,
Or we will stifle in our effluent.
That sort of thing, we're told
Put paid to the dinosaurs—
Lumbering Diplododocus, leggy Iguanodon,
Baroque Triceratops and Stegosaur—
Our childhood friends, or the earth's childhood.
And that will be the ultimate news from nowhere—
For us and our computers.

Some find it reassuring to suppose
An elvish folk will land—
Grass-green men from outer space,
Or from the hollow centre of the earth,—
In delicate porcelain flying saucers—
Peter Pan or Noddy at their head.

Lob-lie-by-the-fire will tidy up our muddle—
It is his metier.

After Götterdämmerung, the Nordic myth recounted,
Baldr returns and his companions—
Beautiful gods who died and were forgotten.
Then in the scorched grass, they'll find the golden chessmen
That they had played with once
Before the first creation of the world.

John Heath-Stubbs

Back

We'd guessed already, of course—pressing between
the unruly hedgerows up lanes whose surface crumbled
beneath our boots; or stumbling
through bracken when the lanes gave out. And yes,
the signs were everywhere—the herds
of feral cattle on the hillsides, tractors
resting in smothered gateways, the blank
stare of deserted farmsteads; but nothing
spooked us like the choughs, the dark hordes lifting
from the cliffs at our approach to wheel and cry
above our heads. We stood
in the fading light and listened to the breakers
hammering the rocks below us; heard the ousted
spirits sweeping back to claim their own.

Jem Poster

Evolution

Why do I linger to watch them dart and pass,
Brilliant slivers unfathomably repeating
Themselves, all they know on their aqueous side of the glass
Among wavering fronds is the throb of gills, and eating.

One speckled gold, with tail like a butterfly's wing;
Some hooped red white black; and there a serrated sail
Like something cut from black crêpe is hovering;
Others are lost in their lace of fins and tail.

There are paper-thin translucencies, filaments
Of life, yet every organ intact. So what
Evolutionary imperatives make sense
Of such miniature perfectedness? It cannot

Be for concealment, such consummate display
Must have to do with courtship; their purpose for ever
Is just to make more of themselves. I turn away,
Strolling back out to the city, where our clever

Species bustles among what it's erected
Since, fin-and-wing-less, perhaps a million years
Ago it rose staggeringly upright. Traffic-infected
Air corrodes churches, chainstores, concrete tiers

Of parking — ornately bizarre as our grandest conceit
Of what we are, politician, professor, priest, poet;
Our courtships riddled with notions of love that defeat
Its fruition; inventions destroying earth as we know it.

And wondering what in nature explains, I think
Of that phosphorescent violet fish that, turning,
Vanished edge-on then flashed again — like a wink
From depths of inscrutable creative yearning.

Andrew Waterman

Front Lines

The edge of the cancer
Swells against the hill—we feel
      a foul breeze—
And it sinks back down.
The deer winter here
A chainsaw growls in the gorge.

Ten wet days and the log trucks stop,
The trees breathe.
Sunday the 4-wheel jeep of the
Realty Company brings in
Landseekers, lookers, they say
To the land,
Spread your legs.

The jets crack sound overhead, it's OK here;
Every pulse of the rot at the heart
In the sick fat veins of Amerika
Pushes the edge up closer—

A bulldozer grinding and slobbering
Sideslipping and belching on top of
The skinned-up bodies of still-live bushes
In the pay of a man
From town.

Behind is a forest that goes to the Arctic
And a desert that still belongs to the Piute
And here we must draw
Our line.

Gary Snyder

The Living World

Homo sapiens is a brilliant and proud citizen
of the biosphere, but Earth is where we
originated and will stay. Who are we to
destroy the planet's Creation? Each species
around us is a masterpiece of evolution,
exquisitely adapted to its environment.

Edward O. Wilson

Grebes

I intersected with in their seasonal
permutations—a reservoir's green flat,
a male bird with the arched back of a cat,

displaying its chestnut ruffs, puffed head-dress,
sharp profiled, red-eyed, gone without a trace
until it corkscrewed back to the surface,

then faced its partner, bill loaded with weed,
head shaking, presenting its courtship gift,
both gratified then resuming their drift

out to opposing dives. A day of mist,
I heard the panic of the fledglings, sharp
falsettos—the mist was strings of a harp

vibrating in the gold light burning through.
Cygnet-style, one fledgling rode on the back
of a parent bird, the other held tack

close by the adult's plumage. Cutting silk,
they moved out to an island; I would watch,
the unpredictable plot of their catch,

the male bird's ever widening radius.
Then winter, I would find them for a week
of storms sheltering in a tidal creek,

or round the coast, seen from a harbour wall,
low on the water, while a lowering grey
rampart of snow clouds packed above the bay.

Jeremy Reed

Bewick Swans Arrive at Ouse Washes

Just when I think winter has won,
a black book closing

on pages of light,
and the darkness sways on its haunches

like an impatient bear
scooping up silver minnows,

I sense an agitation in the sky,
long Vs trailing like pennons.

Altocirrus, the swans are as white
as the tundra they come from.

Their cries multiply. Their bodies
crash-land on the water

star after star after star.

Lynne Wycherley

Curlew

The curve of its cry—
A sculpture
Of the long beak:
A spiral carved from bone.

It is raised
       quickening
From the ground,
Is wound high, and again unwound,
      down
To the stalker nodding
In a marshy field.

It is the welling
Of a cold mineral spring,
Salt from the estuary
Dissolved, sharpening
The fresh vein bubbling on stone.

It is an echo
Repeating an echo
That calls you back.

It looses
Words from dust till the live tongue
Cry: This is mine
Not mine, this life
Welling from springs
Under ground, spiralling
Up the long flight of bone.

Jeremy Hooker

Hawks

Hawks hovering, calling to each other
      Across the air, seem swung
Too high on the risen wind
      For the earth-clung contact of our world:
And yet we share with them that sense
      The season is bringing in, of all
The lengthening light is promising to exact
      From the obduracy of March. The pair,
After their kind are lovers and their cries
      Such as lovers alone exchange, and we
Though we cannot tell what it is they say,
      Caught up into their calling, are in their sway,
And ride where we cannot climb the steep
      And altering air, breathing the sweetness
Of our own excess, till we are kinned
      By space we never thought to enter
On capable wings to such reaches of desire.

Charles Tomlinson

A Sparrow-Hawk in the Suburbs

At that time of year there is a turn in the road where
the hermit tones and meadow colours of
two seasons heal into
one another.

When the wild ladder of a winter scarf is stored away in
a drawer eased by candle-grease and lemon balm
is shaken out from
the linen press.

Those are afternoons when the Dublin hills are so close,
so mauve and blue, we can be certain dark
will bring rain and
it does to

the borrowed shears and the love-seat in the garden where
a sparrow hawk was seen through the opal-
white of apple trees
after Easter. And

I want to know how it happened that those days of bloom when
rumours of wings and sightings — always seen by
someone else, somewhere else —
filled the air,

together with a citrus drizzle of petals and clematis opening,
and shadows waiting on a gradual lengthening
in the light our children
stayed up

later by, over pages of wolves and dragons and learned to
measure the sanctuary of darkness by a small
danger — how and why
they have chilled

into these April nights I lie awake listening for wings I will
never see above the cold frames and
last frosts of our
back gardens.

Eavan Boland

Barn Owl at Le Chai

Tonight, cooling off on the terrace,
glow-worms lighting the long grass,
we listen for crickets, nightingales, nightjars,
turning our palms to the first stars.
Little mists rise in the night garden,
then, a shriek of something taken,
and in the darkness under the trees, white
flowers, feathers, her cry in flight,
and the air is blood-flecked,
a grief in retrospect.

Gillian Clarke

Swallows

For five successive days they've opened out
into the drilling rain, twitchy zigzags
of bat-loops, aerial curvatures that trace
a frenetic flight-line on space,
the crack of their wings snapping like blue flags
cuffed by a gust, streamlined, putting to rout
the sluggish insect traffic, a slow bee
stumbling on a cold-level energy.

I thought they'd done, the fields stubbled red-gold,
a wet September, but their eager cries
were chasing, harrying from tree to ground,
in search of what they hadn't found,
the overreach that has them desert ties,
a black arc beating sunwards from the cold,
delayed here, frisking across a meadow
with such industry you can feel the flow

of current, surcharge in the beady eye.
I watched them from a flapping chestnut grove,
scything the air-currents, a huddled stain
of crows facing into the rain,
tireless, wing-feeding, now dipping above
the plankton-line, embroidering the sky
with spirals, helices, darting to catch
a brittle wasp that sputters like a match.

Jeremy Reed

The Blackbird

One morning in the month of June
I was coming out of this door
And found myself in a garden,
A sanctuary of light and air
Transplanted from the Hesperides,
No sound of machinery anywhere,
When from a bramble bush a hidden
Blackbird suddenly gave tongue,
Its diffident, resilient song
Breaking the silence of the seas.

Derek Mahon

On a Dropped Feather

Until the feather tapers like an arrow
it's a stem of hollow smoky glass
unsnappable from root to subtle tip.
A grounded starling could survive the loss.
This ferny plumage where the shaft begins
is made of down too delicate for flight,
unlike the finny structure of the outer wing,
fashioned for soaring. Perhaps the taut
intrinsic music of a bird comes
from the staves on its small fledged limbs.
The feather's utmost fibres have all the colour
and congruence of shot silk. From the loud strife
and beating of wings in the sky somewhere
it fell like the notched blade of a knife.

Catrióne O'Reilly

Badger

for Raymond Piper

I

Pushing the wedge of his body
Between cromlech and stone circle,
He excavates down mine shafts
And back into the depths of the hill.

His path straight and narrow
And not like the fox's zig-zags,
The arc of the hare who leaves
A silhouette on the sky line.

Night's silence around his shoulders,
His face lit by the moon, he
Manages the earth with his paws,
Returns underground to die.

II

An intestine taking in
patches of dog's-mercury,
brambles, the bluebell wood;
a heel revolving acorns;
a head with a price on it
brushing cuckoo-spit, goose-grass;
a name that parishes borrow.

III

For the digger, the earth-dog
It is a difficult delivery
Once the tongs take hold,

Vulnerable his pig's snout
That lifted cow-pats for beetles,
Hedgehogs for the soft meat,

His limbs dragging after them
So many stones turned over,
The trees they tilted.

Michael Longley

The Cheetah

So here they are, what above all
        You've longed to see — the cheetahs.
Earth's swiftest beast, its speed exceeds
        One hundred kilometres

An hour. They lope or laze, strong tails
        For turning in mid-chase
Twitch idly. Born to run, they know
        It's pointless in this place.

One briefly scampers at a trot
        To hint what it might do;
From instinct cubs play stalking games
        Though born inside this zoo.

Another pads to the wire-mesh,
        Pauses. Eyes meet. We see
Crisp rippling sandy fur, black spots,
        He views us patiently,

Neither as prey, nor threat; has seen
        So often the likes of us.
Our camera clicks, he flicks away.
        And we go for our bus.

When in your sleep's wide plains a gold
        Streak veers, coils, springs, eyes slits,
Is it the cheetah treads your dream,
        Or you who've entered its?

Andrew Waterman

The Fox

When I saw the fox, it was kneeling
in snow: there was nothing to confess
that, tipped on its broken forepaws
the thing was dead—save for its stillness.

A drift, confronting me, leaned down
across the hill-top field. The wind
had scarped it into a pennine wholly of snow, and
where did the hill go now?

There was no way round
I drew booted legs
back our of it, took to my tracks again,
but already a million blown snow-motes were
flowing and filling them in.

Domed at the summit, then tapering,
the drift still mocked
my mind as if the whole
fox-infested hill were the skull of a fox.

Scallops and dips
of pure pile rippled and shone, but what
should I do with such beauty
eyed by that?

It was like clambering between its white temples
as the crosswind tore
at one's knees, and each
missed step was a plunge at the hill's blinding interior.

Charles Tomlinson

Snake

Snake lazing in the wet grass,
less useful than cow or horse.

Line of silver on the family path,
silver as the Rio de la Plata.

Serpent silver as my ring, my bracelet,
laughing silently as those two circles.

Serpent tingling from place to place,
one of those who do not save lives,

at whom the countrywomen fling sharp stones,
but whose daughters greet with sudden smiles.

Creature more magic than mouse or rat,
more thoughtful than donkey or cat,

whose cry is mistaken for wind in the trees,
from whom so much has been stripped,

now you are only one limb,
one skein, one thumb,

you are a long thin silver skin,
a rod that works for god.

Because of your perfection
we say you possess venom and deceit

but whoever has perfection
can do without compassion.

Silver female with your nest of pure white eggs,
you live both by basking and gliding,

you die without screaming,
you come to an end,

your silver stiffening to pewter,
then thawing back into the shallows of earth.

Your young wriggle free,
bruised but seamless,
each one her own stepping stone.

Penelope Shuttle

The Peacock

Michaelmas daisy, latest flower
  To tempt the old sun and new frost,
Glows by the wood a final hour
  Before the heat of day is lost

And one drab peacock butterfly
  Drifts through the sharp October light,
To quiver notched and faded wings
  Leafbrown against the mauveish white.

Its summer namesake was a bird,
  Emblem of watchfulness and pride;
But time has left the name absurd—
  Worn, perforated, shadow-eyed,

The brittle traveller takes her rest,
  Nuzzles the flowers to find her food,
And has some hours to live at best;
  Night, cold and death are in the wood.

Stubborn survivor, in a cloak
  Like a torn carpet stained with dust
And wine and dew and battle-smoke,
  The peacock drags her gold and rust

And clambers on the anther-tips:
  Her happiness gleams rich and dull.
I share the pungent taste she sips;
  The flowers of death and life are full.

Grevel Lindop

Moths

Tonight the air smells of cut grass.
Apples rust on the branches. Already summer is
a place mislaid between expectation and memory.

This has been a summer of moths.
Their moment of truth comes well after dark.
Then they reveal themselves at our window-
ledges and sills as a pinpoint. A glimmer.

The books I look up about them are full of legends:
ghost-swift moths with their dancing assemblies at dusk.
Their courtship swarms. How some kinds may steer by the moon.

The moon is up. The back windows are wide open.
Mid-July light fills the neighbourhood. I stand by the hedge.

Once again they are near the windowsill—
fluttering past the fuchsia and the lavender,
which is knee-high, and too blue to warn them

they will fall down without knowing how
or why what they steered by became, suddenly,
what they crackled and burned around. They will perish—

I am perishing—on the edge and at the threshold of
the moment all nature fears and tends towards:

the stealing of the light. Ingenious facsimile.

And the kitchen bulb which beckons them makes
my child's shadow longer than my own.

Eavan Boland

Daddy-Long-Legs

It was an act of daring then to fling one at the girls,
a kind of modest proposal like requesting the pleasure
of a dance, and their cries, we understood, were pleasure.

Purring and rattling in the palms then out upon the world—
flop-flop across benches and the grass, these maddened ghosts
had their legs broken or pulled off, silent in their pain.

Little brown handkerchiefs animated by bluff currents,
blowing against windows where a veil of condensation
held back the damp larders of grass, bark, potato-leaf.

Those days were shorter. Our legs froze although properly speaking
it was hardly autumn. The television lay muzzled in
the front room. Tap and splay. They hung there, vegetal.

God save these daddies and all their young babies—
repulsive fry greasing the cellar, leathery nuisance.
Put salt on them like slugs, their curling slime.

They lilt against the lightbulb, out of control: in hell
they will be gorged with our blood, now they are brittle
girls proffering leaves and hands, ragged, memorial.

George Szirtes

Dragonfly

Bullet of stained glass glancing out of the traffic.
Some trembling cellophane I find at my feet.
Handspan of colours; daubs from the palette of light.
Black honeycomb pattern embroidered on wings.
Carnage in October: blue scalds of the dusk.
Somnolent. Extinguished. Jewel of pus on dragonfly snout.
I hold in my hand a crucifix on the Cribwr road.

Robert Minhinnick

The Green Aphis

Who made the little aphis,
    The plump green fly,
Strong enough to walk beneath
    The tonnage of the sky?

Who made his bent and trembling legs,
    Gingerly and thin,
Withstand the onrush of creation
    Rushing down on him?

Who made his soft adhesive feet
    Tread with certainty
Along my gently shaking hand
    Unafraid of me?

A life of careful learning
    All men understand
Can teach me only that he moves
    At God's command.

Sebastian Barker

The Eel

The eel, that cold-water siren
migrating from the Baltic
to our warm Mediterranean,
is streamlined to resist the flood
in foment, and keeps low, its quick
malleable pokerhead, snaking
from hairline to hairline crevice,
working upstream, so sinuous
it might pass through a wedding ring,
at last reaches the coppered light
filtering through green chestnut trees
and lies there, fired to a tabby
cat's orange markings in water
slowed from rivulets that streak across
the Apennines to the Romagna;
and contorted to a whiplash
catches fire like a pitch-arrow
in the arid craters left by
drought where mosquitoes simmer,
suddenly adopts the storm glow
of a spark that points to how
embers quicken in their extinction
round the stump of a dead tree-bole,
and how the brief, iridescent
blazing of its tornado flash,
is twin to the one between your eyes,
mad sister finding like a moth
ecstasy in the flame's surprise.

Jeremy Reed

Landscapes
and Inscapes

And just as surely as we are physically
shaped for this world of nature, so too are we
psychically made for it, and this symbiosis
of nature and the human psyche is genetically
coded as surely as our colour vision and the
shape of our hands and face. It is not
something we can shake off, a skin we have
out-grown, but something that is built into our
genes over the millions of years during which
our humanity evolved.

John Feehan

The End of the World

"We're going," they said, "to the end of the world".
So they stopped the car where the river curled,
And we scrambled down beneath the bridge
On the gravel track of a narrow ridge.

We tramped for miles on a wooded walk
Where dog-hobble grew on its twisted stalk.
Then we stopped to rest on the pine-needle floor
While two ospreys watched from an oak by the shore.

We came to a bend, where the river grew wide
And green mountains rose on the opposite side.
My guides moved back. I stood alone,
As the current streaked over smooth flat stone.

Shelf by stone shelf the river fell.
The white water goosetailed with eddying swell.
Faster and louder the current dropped
Till it reached a cliff, and the trail stopped.

I stood at the edge where the mist ascended,
My journey done where the world ended.
I looked downstream. There was nothing but sky,
The sound of the water, and the water's reply.

Dana Gioia

Amazonas

Straight up out of the Pacific
grooves of rock that peak the clouds with ice
splinter into rivers running East.
Cloud-forests melting in July,
the Amazon at its source,
jungle of island-fringes a horizon
dividing water and sky: two azures,
evolving soft ephemera of trees
through which monkeys crash, birds cry out,
howls liquefy, great white egrets
coil downward into extreme sculpture.
Here is where the river begins to move
headlong at terrible speed
into the earth.

Thrilling with Andes snow
delivering rainclouds, fruit, vines, water,
the vast drainage of Amazon seeks every outlet
inlet and lake, and moves through it
sometimes will not move
sometimes like to drift in a still depth fringed
by insect-floating growth, peacock fish
slothlike green canopies of trees.
But will reach salt water.
Dying into the earth's future.
Amazonas — living with its trees a few million years
together in their best of times secretly.

Alert to floating damage, torn-off roots
the shaman steers crouched,
a human rudder,
then in a liquid wilderness of glints
steering us through needles of black palm,
knowing where the simple secrets grow
trance-inducing vines,
eyes like beetles running among leaves
where trees flower —

So that night we drank his drug of bark
growing in our ears the drumming
of millions of insects, nightjars, frogs,
seemed like a city's steady traffic hum
heard from an open skylight or a street,
all sound vacuumed from the trees
into a jet of planet-circling air,
as over mountains our small plane
broke through the seal of mist
into a wide entrance of green heat,
rivers coiled like empty asphalt tracks.

Father and son
—steering words,
moving upstream.
Alligator eyes
caught red in flash-beams in the reeds.
Upstream to the coolness of our camp.
The moment being given to us again—
that we were here and saw the rim of the galaxy,
a shapely arc,
huts on the shores,
after-sunset handling of nets,
all of it blowing through us gusts of elation,
sharp joy—
the Milky Way,
slant of the Southern Cross,
riding in that boat against the wind.

Paul Mills

The Oregon Coast

I

This half-ruined porch of giants,
rough men of granite and basalt
grown hairy with hemlock and fur.

They sit looking down through storms,
forming some dark, volcanic thought,
their only speech the sound of waves
crashing against their knees.

The green pillars of their temple
topple behind them; sunlight
leans on the sprawled columns,
and sheep crop the gutted floors.

II

The centuries unroll in free-falling
loops of stone. Now and then a giant
pitches from his loosened chair,
the ocean grows heavy with evening,
night closes the small white look
of alders among the ferns.

Long after, in the levelled wreck
of California,
I remembered the inward sweep
of a granite forehead, the drenched
magnificence not yet destroyed.

John Haines

The Bøya Glacier

Eerily blue like a cascade from heaven,
a cold light captured between summers,

it wedges between the sheen of the sky
and shattered grey mountains,
its inching glass suspended over my head.

A sign shouts silently *Danger! Glaciers
are in motion!* I listen for a tell-tale creak
in the depths, the sly creep of death,

as if the Ice Age still looms here,
a blue-grey wolf hunkered on the rocks
easing its weight into August's green glade.

With caution I scan the dank shale at its edge,
black grit of moraine, pink helliborine
startling the snow, meltwater dripping

small coins all day with slow grief,
and I look again at the glacier's height,
the just-glimpsed body of frozen light,

a dying hand flung down the valley,
a sweat of diamonds vanishing as I watch.

Lynne Wycherley

Giant Surf
for Michael Armstrong

We can't locate its place of origin,
this running wall, and its each successor
that breaks a mile out on a reef, then runs

at the gradient of a razor blade,
slightly atilt, and is the pilot wave
of that fomenting wreath of swell that's stayed

by opposition of a barrier,
and gaining momentum flicks the white crest
it inclines vertically, then waterfalls

into the wave's advance, and white water
boils dazzlingly at three times a man's height,
and expends itself in measured thunder

across the wide flat of Atlantic beach,
and in its outgoing rebuffs, but can't
impede, the next wave's towering overreach

that scuttles surfers, who in red and blue
attempt to choreographize each new
breaker's overhang, then fallen, review

the bay's slate-blue corrugations for that
one freak wave climbing to obliterate
the skyline, and on whose crest they'll lie flat,

pinpointing balance, vibrant in the light
of the spray's iridescence, until thrown,
they are towed forward, and surface to fight

the backlash that will wash them out to sea,
and winded, bask awhile in the shallows,
bodies aglow with that salt energy,

as though light formed a film on their torsos,
and left their flesh-tones a beaten silver.
They stand there, twenty of them, flecked with snow,

wading back into breakers, slipping free
into their element, while the sheer air
rings with each new wave's volubility.

Jeremy Reed

Here, at the Tide's Turning

You close your eyes and see
                              the stillness of
the mullet-nibbled arteries, samphire
on the mudflats almost underwater,
and on the saltmarsh whiskers of couch-grass
twitching, waders roosting, sea-lavender
faded to ashes.

            In the dark or almost dark
shapes sit on the staithe muttering of plickplack,
and greenshanks, and zos beds;
                              a duck arrives
in a flap, late for a small pond party.

The small yard's creak and groan and lazy rap,
muffled water music.

                  One sky-streamer,
pale and half-frayed, still dreaming of colour.

Water and earth and air quite integral:
all Waterslain one sombre aquarelle.

From the beginning, and last year, this year,
you can think of no year when you have
not sat on this stub of a salt-eaten stanchion.

Dumbfounded by such tracts of marsh and sky—
the void swirled round you and pressed against you—
you've found a mercy in small stones.

This year, next year, you cannot think
of not returning: not to perch in the blue
hour on this blunt jetty, not to wait, as of right,
for the iron hour and the turning of the tide.

You cross the shillying and the shallows
and, stepping on to the marsh, enter
a wilderness.

Quick wind works around you.

You are engulfed in a wave of blue flames.

No line that is not clear cut and severe,
nothing baroque or bogus. The voices
of young children rehearsing on the staithe
are lifted from another time.

                              This is
battleground. Dark tide fills the winking pulks,
floods the mud-canyons.

        This flux, this anchorage.

Here you watch, you write, you tell the tides.
You walk clean into the possible.

                    Kevin Crossley-Holland

Fens

The flat land was a watery eye
Across it came the dribbled notes of curlews
Lamenting sunset. Occasional herons stood
Up to their knees in blue water
Hunched grey coats on their old men's backs.
The reeds hissed in among the pools
And a quick curve of otter pattered over sand
Dissolved in a deep ring of nothing.
Stars shone weak as pearls and no moon
Climbed into silence.
Only a flagging line of geese in rags
Came down muttering Eskimo on thin water.

                    Kenneth C. Steven

The Black Fens

This land remembers
the grebe's long shadow,
fisher-king.

Bulrushes spell
the shine of water,
dykes slicing to the edge.

Tractors still trail
drift-nets of gulls
on charcoal fields.

Peat has a long memory,
rich black essence
of eight thousand years

shrink-wrapped
in grow-bags,
stripped by the wind,

the true fen shrinking
even as you breathe.
Sometimes I hear

the scream of metal
on frozen wood
cut the horizon:

a bog-oak writhing
out of the dark
into the cold light of now.

Lynne Wycherley

Wood Farm

Clutching this twisted rusty
key, like some furtive gaoler,
I find the back door. Slowly,
the lock unsticks. I enter,
glancing quickly round although
only nettles live here now.

This place lacks the old-house smell
of rotting timber, other
autumns' leaves, and the quick fall
of crumbling plaster. I stare
across the ochre air, drawn
to interminable brown.

The beams creak; the rain gently
taps on a cracked window-pane;
and outside the falling grey
East Anglian afternoon
turns silently to evening
as I wait here wondering

about our pasts and our futures.
Farmers prospered here: their food
graced this oven; their pastures,
lands made heavy with their blood,
are barren now; the soil grows
mere scrub, dead with its owners.

And dead for the future too.
Rest in peace. Let the poppies
colour this place and the dew
shine on the shattered windows,
reflecting through slow decay
a natural dignity.

Neil Powell

The Twist in the River

At the clear, beer-coloured and bubbleshot twist in the river—
Every stone a speckled egg spawned in that deep lap,
Every pockmarked, pitted pebble a planet, blindly seeing through its
      own evolution—
The shallows, the tall air, are filled with sound and light.
This part of the river expects to be seen, for it has drawn you there,
And the trees, selfless, introduce the sky into your love for the water.
If this place were a person, it would be making up a paper hat while
      humming,
Entirely self-contained, absorbed yet radiant—
A family moment, appearing normal until years later in retrospect,
When its depths are fully felt, beyond blunt experience.

Underwater, the light thickens slightly but never sets
And the river runs through its own fingers, careless.

Katherine Pierpoint

To the Edge

To the scatter of a hamlet where nothing happens,
slowly. Sixty generations banked in the mud of
dogged minds.

To the scruffy hem of a rhomboid: acres torched and
charred. And far off as childhood the boy with
Punch and plough now a man astride his scarlet tractor.
Trawler of a torque of yelping gulls.

To the bounding lane. Skimmed and lumpen. Spinning
balls of gnats; matted honeysuckle. Acid in the
elderflower, old-fashioned Albertines athwart an
unhinged gate: those were the days less happy than
we think they were.

To the empty paddock and slat-crusted wall, the glossy
guarded holm-oaks.

To Mother Creek, flowing and flowering: her Byzantine
dark fingers laying open the marsh. The pools and
pulks are orange and sepia and slate-blue. Silt. Salt.
Yap of rigging. All the old arguments.

To a spur that's ragged. Beyond the leaching chemicals
and uprooted hedges, to the crossing-place where soil
and saltmarsh meet.

To a floor of uneven flagstone, filmed with beeswax.
Unfounded. Well-trodden. Flanked by clods of flint,
rough lime mortar.

Look at sun's fierce lances, the dance of light on
stone: word and spirit have reached an agreement.

The smell of mud and rose. You know you can still
tune this world: the way the mind infiltrates, ideas
assemble as if of themselves; the heart's pluck;
ancient, inner voices.

To an innocent page, damp and salty, and this fitful pen.

To the edge that's always chill and uncomfortable.
Tall reeds sing in the ditch. Tide turns against
the wind, bucking and amber and hilarious.

Kevin Crossley-Holland

Garra Rock

And the end and the beginning were always there
Before the beginning and after the end.
T.S. Eliot

We must remember: *All is always now.*
So, today I'm at Garra Rock—the steep jag of descent,
Us clambering down.
I hear your *Look! Look!* wind-slung to the horizon;
See the gannets' perfect plumb-line drop—
Perpendicular flight programmed for their constant dive.

Generation after generation genes go on
Repeating themselves. Coded chromosomes,
Nucleic acids, proteins, enzymes, ribosomes
Generation after generation . . . go on . . . go on . . .

Here, now . . . always now: the boy paddling with his father.
And you, arms akimbo, remarking,
How alike they seem:
Same shoulder droop, squat stance, pallid flesh,
Shortened arc from neck to head.
Life to come fixed a million years before any one life has begun.

Quick now, here —
Now your son, only four then, cautious, skirting the water's edge.
You, cross-armed, longing to plunge like gannets headfirst in.
Generation after generation —
Me, exultant (my parents taught me how to swim),
Leaping in the toss and drag
Of that day's sea-wind convulsion.

Generation after generation genes go on
Repeating themselves. Coded chromosomes,
Nucleic acids, proteins, enzymes, ribosomes
Go on . . . go on . . .

And can you see the frenzy —
Drenched towels, a soaked sandal, your book being flung,
When an errant tidal tongue, as it has always done,
Hurls the blueprint of the future in?
Yet though that day years ago has gone,
The salt stain on our lives then —
Here, now, quick — immediate.

Lisa Dart

The South Downs

Long before names, before we thought of naming,
seas roared through, dividing Sussex Downs
from what is France; carving through millennia
of laid down life, this chalk, these flints, the land
we came to know as home. Long before that
the cosmos dreamed of consciousness, filled space
with elements that one day would lead to us.

Now every grain of soil, each artifact,
the air we breathe, the sweep of shadowed grass,
directly links us with our common birth
and every crafted work, each photograph,
each stone we gather from a storm-washed beach,
points always back, reminds us of the time
it took to get here, step by step.

Ted Walter

Below Cym Bychan

There was nothing to be said about
the sky or the clouds that drifted there;
the oaks were all that oaks should be:
sun splashed itself through foliage.

A stream ran on between rocks, clear,
water impelled by water, gushing,
bustling with the noise that water makes
          when it is free.
Trout slit the glass of a deeper pool;
a dragonfly skimmed its clarity;
a waterboatman sculled between stones.

Birds conversed among branches, hidden,
and children's cries range in the trees
remotely, caught and held as if
in a green and greener dream of leaves.

Richard Poole

Sap

Where the stream ox-bowed
And we stood on a bulwark
Of planks and turf, the current
Made its darkest passage,
A black stillwater, treacherous
Beneath a sheen of scum.

Once, and once only, a trout rose,
Its lean sides gleaming like
A knife between the stones,
Crimson shadow at its belly.
Yet how often was the only sound
Not the Ffornwg or our
White thrash after fish,
But the thinnest flute of the sap
Maintaining its single note
A long minute in my head
As I imagined that pressure
Of water rising through the trees,
Streams moving vertically
And spilling in a silent turbulence
Along the boughs, a river
Flowing there beneath the bark,
The sap, singing, even as flesh
Leaned white and stunned
Against the visible current,
And the gwrachen like a small
Green stick swam past the hand.

Robert Minhinnick

Everything Comes out of the Cool Dark Mine

Cars in gridlock
  trains running on time
    or not
Buggies for all colours of babies
  paperclips for holding tax forms insecurely
    canteens of cutlery
Buckles for belts controlling paunches
  brass bands blowing through copper, zinc
    Operating theatres
all alert
  buckets for kicking
    hub-caps and dog chains
Artificial knee-caps
  Bronze Age weapons
    Iron Age Culture
Copper, tin, zinc, lead
  All keys to the locks, and locks to the keys
    The F.A. Cup,
that Holy Grail
  The Minister's collar-stud
    the priest's glittering plate
and his pipe church organ of tin
  the tooth fillings for speech
    Razor blades
And bootlace-tips
  spades that are spades
    mousetraps and spectacle frames
The whole orchestra
  from piccolo
    to big bass drum's
shining brass fitting
  Nose-rings for hefting bulls
    winter radiators that hiss
like snakes,
  Kazoos, binoculars
    All the news fit to print
Frontdoor bells,
  cathedral bells,
    Guns and javelins,
eyebrow tweezers
  rheumatism bracelets,

                    the winding in copper wire
of all London's electricity,
            bathtaps that gleam and refresh,
                    satellite dishes, hairpins,
scissors, the whole of Nasa,
            the water-dam over there,
                    and more to come
Try it yourself from those tunes
            (in music,
                    "the harmonious rhythmic tremor
of the union of copper and tin . . .")
            gongs, horns, organ pipes,
                    copper, iron, zinc, silver . . .

                                    Peter Redgrove

Song

The deep gabble and
            deafening groan of the Work
                    done with the great
Rotation drums, the howl of the mine,
            the oratory of the mine
                    the conversable mine
In the Mill, their fitness
            to be Crushers, Sieves, Filters,
                    slime-syrup cleaners
The polyglot of the mine
            mill-labyrinth of implements
                    and organs of extraction
Huge and less huge but none small
            the landscape of down-there speaking
                    Tin, copper, zinc,
silver, silver, copper
            The great fields of copper,
                    silver, tin, silver
zinc, copper, tin, tin tin
            Jane Jane Jane
                    Yein Yein Yein
Yoni of water, ladderless depths

                                    Peter Redgrove

Topsoil

I walk these moors for what they are.
The wind's runways. It swoops
Whoo-ing in my ears like sad owls,
Their beaks at my face where
The scarf can't cover. Beyond them
Curlews, constantly panicking,
Calling away from invisible nests.

This is the sky's full drop.
It doesn't have to cramp around cities
Or spear itself on spires.
Here it can stretch down its legs
And walk. It strides over the heather
Farther than I can see. The curlews
Call between its knees.

I walk these moors for what they are.
Neglected roof gardens of the mill towns
Left to fend for themselves, riding
The landscape with a small burden of sheep
And Sunday walkers. Where purple flowers
Tongue a late summer bell
Pealing low blue notes.

The marsh sucks my feet to a certain depth
And no further. The old sheep tracks lie
Deep down with monks' footprints.
Below, an Iron Age prospector once scratched
For ore, plundered trees for his furnace,
And below, a Bronze Age shepherd
Slept beneath them.

It matters little that the Vikings came
Or the Romans landed. That once this
Vast scar of heath was solid ice
Or fertile forest. The peat preserves
Old seeds: all swallowed now and
Well digested. I walk these moors
For what they are.

Robyn Bolam

Landscape

Here my imagination
Tangles through a turfstack
Like skeins of sheep's wool:
Is a bull's horn silting
With powdery seashells.

I am clothed, unclothed
By racing cloud shadows,
Or else disintegrate
Like a hillside neighbour
Erased by sea mist.

A place of dispersals
Where the wind fractures
Flight-feathers, insect wings
And rips thought to tatters
Like a fuchsia petal.

For seconds, dawn or dusk,
The sun's at an angle
To read inscriptions by:
The splay of the badger
And the otter's skidmarks

Melting into water
Where a minnow flashes:
A mouth drawn to a mouth
Digests the glass between
Me and my reflection.

Michael Longley

After the Storm

Waters come welling into this valley
　　From a hundred sources. Some
Sealed by the August heat, dry back
　　From a dusty bed and only when the leaves
Are down again, rustle and rush
　　In their teeming gulley after the storm.

Today—just once—the sun looks forth
    To catch the misty emanations of our north
Rising in spirals underneath the hill:
    Here, like a steaming beast, a house
Emerges into its beams, the mist
    Smoking along them into a vapour veil
That trails up into soaked branches
    Sending down shower on shower
The sky is clear for an hour. Where the sun
    Is going under it seems to impose
That silence against which the streams keep telling
    Over and over in the ebbing light
In their voices of liquid suasion, of travelling thunder
    From what depths they have drunk and from what heights.

Charles Tomlinson

Orchard with Wasps

The rouged fruits in
The orchard by the waterfall, the bronzed fruits,

The brassy flush on the apples.
He gripped the fruit

And it buzzed like a gong stilled with his fingers
And a wasp flew out with its note

From the gong of sugar and scented rain
All the gongs shining like big rain under the trees

Within the sound of the little waterfall
Like a gash in the apple-flesh of time

Streaming with its juices and bruised.
Such a wasp, so full of sugar

Flew out within the sound
Of the apple-scented waterfall,

Such a gondola of yellow rooms
Striped with black rooms

Fuelled with syrups hovering
At the point of crystal,

Applegenius, loverwasp, scimitar
Of scented air and sugar-energy

Shining up his lamp-tree tall and devious
Given utterly to its transformations

From sharp-scented flowers to honey-gongs,
Giver and taker of pollination-favours,

A small price for such syrups and plunderings,
Its barky flesh, its beckoning fruit,

Its deep odour of cider and withering grasses,
Its brassy bottles and its Aladdin gold-black drunks.

Peter Redgrove

Point No Point

Why name a place Point No Point?

Does it mean we are nowhere
when we reach it?

Does it mean we lose our sense
of meaning, our sense of direction
when we stop at Point No Point?

Begin again, add
that it was the place we almost missed,
and then it was the place we returned to
        again and again
braking at the abrupt dirt road detour—

Hidden by trees, entangled
        in disagreements,
        we found shelter, a view—
a clearing that was not a clearing.

Why name a place Point No Point?
In any case, here we are, you said,
in a new landscape—will it change your mind?
Here we are
in a game called 'begin at zero'—
how many lighthouses can you love
without fainting?
And can you find enough
pine trees to define the infinite dark green?
If zero is love on the way to the lighthouse
then where is the balance?
And will it change your mind?
Will the sky provide a clue to your confusion?

Well, here we are, you said, now try
to understand the Juan de Fuca Strait.

Begin again, remember
once we stopped for no reason,
back-tracked down to Point No Point
for no reason except that the light
was sudden—it pulled us in,
          kept us still.

Then, just when we thought it was time
to leave, we saw them:
a group of orcas in the distance—seven,
maybe eight—they were swimming towards us—

black and white, and black and white
their rising and falling: generous, endless
          black and white, thy burned—
it was their bodies that made
          the waves alert—
it was the largeness of their yearning, an innocent
          violence spinning within their grace—
black and white, and black and white
the surface: muscular, turbulent—It was more
than passion,   more
                    that made our blood learn—

that made our blood learn.

Sujata Bhatt

The Home
of Experience

Man is indispensable for the completion of
creation; he himself is the second creator of the
world, who alone has given to the world its
objective existence—without which, unheard,
unseen, silently eating, giving birth, dying,
heads nodding through hundreds of millions of
years, it would have gone on in the profoundest
night of non-being down to its unknown end.

Carl Jung

This Moment

A neighbourhood.
At dusk.

Things are getting ready
to happen
out of sight.

Stars and moths.
And rinds slanting around fruit.

But not yet.

One tree is black.
One window is yellow as butter.

A woman leans down to catch a child
who has run into her arms
this moment.

Stars rise.
Moths flutter.
Apples sweeten in the dark.

Eavan Boland

Things

What I'll miss most when I'm dead is
things that the light shines on.
If there aren't wet leaves in Heaven
then almost I don't want to go there.
If there isn't the possibility
of silly particulars
like library cards on a table
then I almost don't want to go there.
Library cards—because here some happen to be.
I am a small Englishman in an infinite Universe
looking at library cards. That's funny.
In fact it frightens me.

I am in my room, surrounded by the things
which have somehow clung to my existence;
a picture of squirrels, a desk with inkstains
(it was my grandfather's before me),
a Buddha and a jar of Nivea,
a pottery lion lying among rosepetals.
These are my things. They comfort
and encumber me.

But Buddha, what about you?
Your sides are so sheer.
You gave all your riches away.
And can you still hold
on to yourself as a person?

Did Christ give up his things too?
He had a seamless garment.
The other things came when he needed them,
a coin in a fish's mouth,
ointment for his feet,
a crown of thorns.
Well, he didn't despise things.
He ate bread readily.
He loved the boats of his disciples.

And it's not just things that we love
but one thing next to another—
this African Violet beside the tuning fork,

this pen in my hand
as the rain outside falls among Quinces.
These things have happened before;
but when I happen to be there
and notice the shape of the space between them
then a new thing arises in the Universe.
This was unplanned.
This event without karma.

Angels, though infinitely greater than us,
know nothing of this.
But Christ knows it.
He came for that purpose —
to write on a particular ground
with his little finger.

The Gods have enough of immortality
and need things.
They need cuckoos in a Damson tree,
they need Rhubarb flapping beside a gate.
Their paternoster is an honest man
who can hammer a nail straight.

Paul Matthews

Horse Chestnuts

The wood was steaming with high summer rain;
grape-white, the light was filtered through the trees
so densely massed it seemed we stood beneath
a green cupola, so imperviously

interleaved, that the rain was gravel whipped
against a tarpaulin, the shuck of peas
unshelled into a bowl. We stood it out,
hearing with each increase a running sea

slowed by a shingle gradient, and then
in the pauses the big drops shaken down.
The leaves were donkeys' ears, long-pointed tips,
descending like a fountain from the crown,

their white candelabra flowers extinguished
with the month. The wood smelt of hop-sacks flushed
out of a barn, and airing in a yard.
We waited, anticipating the hushed

intervals between showers, caught up now
in the rain's drum-stick tapping, each crystal
a kitten advancing on cellophane.
Was it months later we returned, the fall

of green thorny-oyster pods, split open
to reveal polished nuts littering the ground,
spiny, the green of weed on wharf jetties?
What we had returned for was what we found,

a quality of underwater light,
this time diffused with amber and yellow,
a white sun pouring through interstices,
glinting, luminous, like a vein that flows

perennially through those branches, a light
that would map out the tree's shorn skeleton
in barest winter, and give to its shape
the hard, glazed dignity it would put on.

Jeremy Reed

Flora

A flutter of leaves
And pages open
Where, as my bookmark,
A flower is pressed,

Calyx, filament,
Anther staining
These pictures of me
In waste places

Shadowing sheep-tracks
From seacliff to dunes,
Ditches that drain
The salty marshes,

Naming the outcasts
Where petal and bud
Colour a runnel
Or sodden pasture,

Where bell and bugle,
A starry cluster
Or butterfly wing
Convey me farther

And in memory
And hands deposit
Blue periwinkles,
Meadowsweet, tansy.

Michael Longley

The Florist's at Midnight

Stems bleed into water
    loosening their sugars
        into the dark,

clouding dank water
    stood in zinc buckets
        at the back of the shop.

All night the chill air
    is humid with breath.
        Pools of it mist

from the dark mouths
    of blooms,
        from the agape

of the last arum lily —
    as a snow-white wax shawl
        curls round its throat

cloaking the slim yellow tongue,
    with its promise of pollen,
        solitary, alert.

Packed buckets
    of tulips, of lilies, of dahlias
        spill down from tiered shelving

nailed to the wall.
    Lifted at dawn,
        torn up from their roots

then cloistered in cellophane,
    they are cargoed across continents
        to fade far from home.

How still they are
        now everyone has gone,
                rain printing the tarmac

the streetlights
        in pieces
                on the floor.

Sarah Maguire

Words

The world does not need words. It articulates itself
in sunlight, leaves, and shadows. The stones on the path
are no less real for lying uncatalogued and uncounted.
The fluent leaves speak only the dialect of pure being.
The kiss is still fully itself though no words were spoken.

And one word transforms it into something less or other —
illicit, chaste, perfunctory, conjugal, covert.
Even calling it a *kiss* betrays the fluster of hands
glancing the skin or gripping a shoulder, the slow
arching of neck or knee, the silent touching of tongues.

Yet the stones remain less real to those who cannot
name them, or read the mute syllables graven in silica.
To see a red stone is less than seeing it as jasper —
metamorphic quartz, cousin to the flint the Kiowa
carved as arrowheads. To name is to know and remember.

The sunlight needs no praise piercing the rainclouds,
painting the rocks and leaves with light, then dissolving
each lucent droplet back into the clouds that engendered it.
The daylight needs no praise; and so we praise it always —
greater than ourselves and all the airy words we summon.

Dana Gioia

Dawn

This is the name
for the moment the quiet house
shifts between night and morning.

I sit in my swivel chair
in a room with two views, waiting
to catch it, the very moment.

Behind me the moon moves slowly down.
Before me the sky lightens, and
tree sounds change from frog

to bird. At first
the sun is an orange line
along the housetops.

Then it is a white ball,
and the moon
is gone.

This happens so fast
I've come dawn after dawn
to slow it down, to trap it.

I want to know what it is.
Not scientifically,
but with my whole body.

I want to know the precise moment
today became yesterday;
tomorrow, today. I want to say

I've gone deep enough,
that I've borrowed nothing, that
I've waited. But this is difficult.

I need to know so urgently exactly how
the woman who lies awake at night
becomes the sleeper, then the dreamer,
then the dream. I want to know why

the words I am saying seem to be spoken
by somebody else.

The sun is higher than my window now
and out of sight.
It is still winter.

I have to know what it's like
the moment that ice is not ice anymore
but isn't yet water.

Andrea Hollander Budy

Advent

After the wideawake galaxies
each dawn is glass.
Leavings of the night's kill lie,
twig-bones, ice-feathers,
the ghost of starlight.

Ewes breathe silver.
The rose won't come—
stopped in her tracks.
Everything's particular:
bramble's freehand,

a leaf caught out,
the lawn's journal.
Deep down even the water-table
stiffens its linen,
and horizons pleat in a bucket.

The stars burn out
to starved birds
watching my window,
and one leaf puts up a hand
against infinite light.

Gillian Clarke

April

The sheer grip and the push of it—growth gets
a footledge in the loosest stems, it takes
the litterings of weeds and clocks them round;
your eyeballs bud and alter and you can't
step twice in the same foot—I know a road,
the curve throws it one way and another;
somebody slipped the gears and bucketed slowly
into the hawthorns and his car took root
and in its bonnet now, amazing flowers
appear and fade and quiddify the month;
and us on bicycles—it was so fast
wheeling and turning we were lifted falling,
our blue-sky jackets filling up like vowels . . .
and now we float in the fair blow of springtime,
kingfishers, each astonishing the other
to be a feathered nerve, to take the crack
between the river's excess and the sun's.

Alice Oswald

Lighting the First Fire of Autumn

Here they are, the quartered logs in their wicker
Basket woven of what I take to be
Birch and split willow plaited together,
The copse offering itself for the burning
Indoors, twig against twig, tree within tree.

Rough-cut block capitals of an alphabet
Older than writing: poplar, beech, pine,
Chainsawed joints of the wood bled and dried out
For a year, lodged in the season's calendar,
Their rituals subordinate, now, to mine

As I build the pyre of oak twigs and newsprint
In the middle of the year's first cold morning.
The TV news shows tropical forests on fire,
Drought in east England, and the Midlands flooded,
A crude mosaic of weather that looks like a warning.

St Columcille said he feared death and hell—
But worse, the sound of an axe in a sacred grove.
Now every grove is sacred, and still we burn
Wood at times, for the fire also is sacred
And a house without it like a heart without love

When the world heads into darkness. The heat's core
Will show you again lost faces and glittering forests,
Mountain passes, caverns, an archetypal world
Recited in the twinkling of a dark pupil.
The epic buried inside us never rests:

Fire is the dark secret of the forest.
The green crowns drink sunlight until their dumb
Hearts are glutted with fire. Then, decaying or burning,
Give up whatever they have. A match flares
And the paper ignites. Watch, and the poems will come.

Grevel Lindop

Autumn

The civility of nature overthrown, the badger must fight in the roofless colosseum of the burning woods.

The birds are in flight, and the sky is in flight, raced by as many clouds as there are waves breaking the lakes beneath it.

Does Tristan lie dying starred by the oak leaves? Tristan is on horseback, in search, squat, with narrow eyes, saddleless, burner of cities.

The field mouse that fled from the blade, flattened by wheels, has dried into the shape of a leaf, a minute paper escutcheon whose tail is the leaf stalk.

Yet the worm still gathers its rings together and releases them into motion . . . You too must freeze.

The horses of Attila scatter the shed foliage under the splashed flags of a camp in transit.

A truce: the first rime has not etched the last oak-shocks; the rivermist floats back from the alders and the sun pauses there.

Peace? There will be no peace until the fragility of the mosquito is overcome and the spirals of the infusoria turn to glass in the crystal pond.

These greens are the solace of lakes under a sun which corrodes. They are memorials not to be hoarded.

There will be a truce, but not the truce of the rime with the oak leaf, the mist with the alders, the rust with the sorrel stalk or of the flute with cold.

It will endure? It will endure as long as the frost.

Charles Tomlinson

The Horse Who Loves Me

1
The horse who loves me is strong and unsaddled.
He desires to learn nothing.
He sleeps standing, like a tree.
He lifts dawn on his willing shoulders.

I ride the horse who loves me,
hands twined in his bashful mane,
knees gripping his nut-butter flanks.

The horse who loves me goes on tiptoe,
his hooves tap the fiery earth.
The long leisure of his muzzle pleases me.

His smell is salt and primroses, honeycomb
and furnace. Oh the sweat of his glittering tail!
How he prances studiously, the horse who loves me.

The horse who loves me has no hobby but patience.
He brings me the gift of his honesty.
His big heart beats with love.
Sometimes he openly seeks a wife. But he returns to me.

The horse who loves me is one of the poor of Paradise.
He enjoys Paradise as such a loving horse might,
quietly watching the seven wonders of the night.

2
Look at my horse!
His neatly-plaited snowy tail
hangs like a fine finger between his pearly buttocks.
His name can be Desire, or Brother.

He does not complain of my weight on his back
any more than darkness complains of its loneliness.

The horse who loves me
wields the prick of pain that caps the dart of love.
We gasp at its pang,
then race for the scaled wall of the sky.

The horse who loves me
takes me beyond the lengths grief goes to,
beyond the strides joy makes
beyond the moon and his sister the future.

This heaven-kissing horse of mine
takes me with him to his aerial home.
Below us, roofs grey, fields fade, rivers shiver, pardoned.
I am never coming back.

Penelope Shuttle

The Beech

Blizzards have brought down the beech tree
    That, through twenty years, had served
As landmark or as limit to our walk:
    We sat among its roots when buds
Fruitlike in their profusion tipped the twigs—
    A galaxy of black against a sky that soon
Leaf-layers would shut back. The naked tree
    Commanded, manned the space before it
And beyond, dark lightnings of its branches
    Played above the winter desolation:
It seemed their charge had set the grass alight
    As a low sun shot its fire into the valley
Splitting the shadows open. Today that sun
    Shows you the place uncitadelled,
A wrecked town centred by no spire,
    Scattered and splintered wide. At night
As the wind comes feeling for those boughs
    There is nothing now in the dark of an answering strength,
No form to confront and to attest
    The amplitude of dawning spaces as when
The tower rebuilt itself out of the mist each morning.

Charles Tomlinson

Becoming a Redwood

Stand in a field long enough, and the sounds
start up again. The crickets, the invisible
toad who claims that change is possible,

And all the other life too small to name.
First one, then another, until innumerable
they merge into the single voice of a summer hill.

Yes, it's hard to stand still, hour after hour,
fixed as a fencepost, hearing the steers
snort in the dark pasture, smelling the manure.

And paralysed by the mystery of how a stone
can bear to be a stone, the pain
the grass endures breaking through the earth's crust.

Unimaginable the redwoods on the far hill,
rooted for centuries, the living wood grown tall
and thickened with a hundred thousand days of light.

The old windmill creaks in perfect time
to the wind shaking the miles of pasture grass,
and the last farmhouse light goes off.

Something moves nearby. Coyotes hunt
these hills and packs of feral dogs.
But standing here at night accepts all that.

You are your own pale shadow in the quarter moon,
moving more slowly than the crippled stars,
part of the moonlight as the moonlight falls.

Part of the grass that answers the wind,
part of the midnight's watchfulness that knows
there is no silence but when danger comes.

Dana Gioia

The Drive

The trees attend to the high wind
Laying back their heads
Sweeping low again.

The wind shakes loose their leaves
Which float down through the air
Becoming days.

Hugo Williams

The Apple Shed

It suddenly thunders and the blue cloud
cracks O run for the sheds
in the clap of time . . .

when it flashes and flashes and the tin sky flickers in the
        thick of echoes,
clear the benches, space the apples,
think of the ten quiet trees with their nerves in the air.

The eye of the storm is my own fear . . .

I wouldn't risk a finger out of doors,
not even for a glancing look
to fetch the key that hangs on the nail
to cross the courtyard to the loo and back

twenty paces under a moving cloudslip . . .

        halfway, caught running in a light from heaven,
        I saw myself struck stiff, but it was just
        the grandeur of thunder, the sheer
        impact of the thought that knocked me blind

and now the comfortable dropping sound
of rain as heavy as a shower of apples:

Ribston Pippin, Cox's Orange,
Woolbrook Russet, Sturmer Pippin,

Bramley, Crispin, Margil, Spartan,
Beauty of Bath and Merton Beauty . . .

Put them bright in rows. Tell me
what have our souls been growing all these years
of time taken and rendered back as apples?

Alice Oswald

Apple

Consider the demotic apple
and its black seeds which just now
I spat out into my hand—

grown here in this city garden
where ivy clasps a lichened tree
of unknown lineage, it has

nevertheless, and despite the scab,
all the desired colour, taste and texture
of an apple to commend it—

and see how, in my palm, the future
lies, centuries of jellies, crumbles, pasties,
aeons of *tartes tatin*, charlottes, pies—

here is a millennium of orchards, ice
floes of blossom, a grumbling avalanche
of windfalls, a distant thrum of wasps.

Angela Kirby

Magnolia Tree

Blood-stemmed, the pink buds grow in pairs of claws.
Burying their hardness in a deep sky,
They span into light feathers, plucked upright.

Last spring another woman watched the sight.
Stood at this window, moved throughout the house
Pursued by rain; the pale shadow of wings.

Out there a bird, which she used to feed, sings
For me — forgetful of her kindnesses.
Notes which would have quelled her panicking fear.

Sometimes, at dusk, I think she might appear
Quietly — to watch the claws of her pain
Soften — as they did, into feathers; rain.

Robyn Bolam

Pruning in Frost

Last night, without a sound,
a ghost of a world lay down on a world,

trees like dream-wrecks
corralled with increments of frost.

Found crevices
and wound and wound
the clock-spring cobwebs.

All life's ribbon frozen mid-fling.

Oh I am
stone thumbs,
feet of glass.

Work knocks in me the winter's nail.

I can imagine
Pain, turned heron,
could fly off slowly in a creak of wings.

And I'd be staring, like one of those
cold-holy and granite kings,
getting carved into this effigy of orchard.

Alice Oswald

Driving in Fog

Driving in fog I part the crowded air,
Then the night falls huge and white across the car.

It is as if I stopped believing in the world
The dark conceals, preferring the immense, cold

Flowerings of fog the headlights stain
To dull amber, the solderings of rain

That glisten on the crawling vehicle.
Yet I never seem to break its streaming wall,

Never reach that moment I can rightly say
Here it begins: always it remains a yard away

In the blurred crowding of fields that overhang
The road, the pale entangling yarns

Of my own breath. Here is not the rain's
Assault, the sullen-strange communion

Of the snow. This is no weather but the bland
Present's arrest, for even the trees stand

Like inked letters half-erased. All traffic
Stops. The fog's white sweat gives radiance to the dark.

In a shrunken world I wait for it to pass,
But the fog like countless faces crowds the glass.

Robert Minhinnick

Eclipse of the Moon

Whose shadow's that?

Who walked in the evening
at his own ghost's back?

Who trod in the circle,
left a toe-print on the frozen pond?

Who looked in the mirror
and clouded the glass?

Who snatched the white moth
in his closed fist?

Who drowned
reaching for the coin?

Gillian Clarke

Watching the Perseids: Remembering the Dead

The Perseids go riding softly down:
Hair-streak moths, brushing with faint wings
This audience of stars with sharp, young faces,
Staring our eyes out with such charming brilliance:
Life, set in its ways and constellations,
Which knows its magnitude, its name and status.

These, though, are whispered ones, looked for in August
Or when we trip on dead and dying birthdays,
Drinking a quiet toast at some green Christmas
To those, who, fallen from space and height
No longer reach us with their smoky fingers
Or touch this sheet of water under no moon.

They are the comet's tail we all must pass through
Dreamed out into a trail of Jack O'Lanterns,
A shattered windscreen on the road to nowhere.
We stand in this late dark-room, watch the Master

Swing, his light-pencil, tentative yet certain,
As if calligraphy could tease out meaning,

And, between a huge water, huger sky,
Glimmers of something on the jimp horizon,
There might be pictures, might be conversations.
We wait for last words, ease the rites of passage,
The cold night hung in chains about our questions,
Our black ark swinging lightly to its mooring.

Peter Scupham

Augury

Magnetic winds from the sun pour in
and send our instruments akimbo.
Nothing runs like clockwork now.
As skeletal clouds unwreathe our exposure,
panicky citizens climb ladders to hammer
their roofs on harder. A crackle of static,
and the world's fat face is in shadow.
There are swallow nests under the eaves,
each with a staring cargo: six bronze bibs,
six black-masked, African birds. They dip
and snap the last bees up. A million Ms
foregather with a million others on the sky.
This is the shape that memory takes.
For days they practise flying, then they fly.

Catrióne O'Reilly

The Kingdom that I Left Behind

There was a river with swans.
That's all. Now that they've flown
I can reflect upon a white reflection.

On their pure whiteness I can reflect;
Or, in a moment when I least expect,
They'll glide into the mind serene and perfect.

And indeed forever they glide in the mind
Perfect and unkind
Back there in the kingdom that I left behind.

In the kingdom of my childhood
The river in flood
Carried a fierce perfection I never understood.

I never could understand the savage grace
Of swans reflecting on the water's face.

Paul Matthews

Archangel

My children have never seen it. It was common here
I tell them, twitching aside the brambles, scanning
the trampled clearing. Sweet-wrappers, cans,
the usual debris.

      Perhaps it was somewhere else
I stood that morning, shorts unbuttoned, pissing
into the beaded grasses as the sun
struck through the rainclouds and the clustered florets
glowed yellow as lemons. A stirring
of hidden life around me; a scent of
is it mint? I can't
quite catch it, but it's there, inseparable
from urine and archangel, from the golden light
streaming between the beeches.

I'm on my knees, I'm searching
for a shoot, a stem, a leaf, for whatever rises
fragrant, ammoniac from the moistened earth.

Jem Poster

If the Owl Calls Again

at dusk
from the island in the river,
and it's not too cold,

I'll wait for the moon
to rise,
then take wing and glide
to meet him.

We will not speak,
but hooded against the frost
soar above
the alder flats, searching
with tawny eyes.

And then we'll sit
in the shadowy spruce
and pick the bones
of careless mice,

while the long moon drifts
toward Asia
and the river mutters
in its icy bed.

And when the morning climbs
the limbs
we'll part without a sound,

fulfilled, floating
homeward as
the cold world awakens.

John Haines

Dreaming Birds

The eyes and feathers intermesh.
Descartes said birds were small machines.
A startled starling clattered off
And flew away at that, it screeched
That birds are loops in modern minds,
Weird flights, a mode, a fatal curve
Of values in the air. The thrush

Is proto-sculpture on the lawn,
The SS crow patrolling down
A motorway's hard shoulder struts
At sentry duty. From a pole
A blackbird soloist transmits
Its live performance and the cool
Woods pay to hear him, dark guitars

Are slung there and electric cries
Flash down the alleyways of spruce,
Afforestation's gentlest crop.
The dreamer Kant thought of a dove
That found air fretful and conceived
A purer flight in empty space.
I dream of swifts that soar asleep.

John Powell Ward

Sleep and Spiders

It is too strange to kill.
The symmetry of its eyes,

its eight paired legs askew
on the lintel, exoskeletal

and tiger-striped, all digestion.
It looks sudden but is still

for hours, eyes on stalks,
awaiting news from hair-triggers

that might be legs or fingers
(the whole thing a claw)

come to touch me in sleep—
hammock from which

black shadows seep.
Stars go milky, then go out.

I wake at five to what five is—
a cold blue glow and a self

trussed, barely breathing,
paralytic with dreams.

Catrióne O'Reilly

Endangered Species

No wonder we love the whales. Do they not carry
Our warm blood below and we remember
Falling asleep in a feeling element
And our voices beating a musical way

To a larger kindred, around the world? Mostly
We wake too quickly, the sleep runs off our heads
And we are employed at once in the usual
Coveting and schemes. I was luckier today

And remembered leaving a house in the Dales
Like home for a night, the four under one roof,
I left them sleeping without a moon or stars
And followed my dreaming self along a road.

Daylight augmented in a fine rain.
I had the sensation of dawning on my face.
But for the animals (and they had gathered
The dark standing in fields and now appeared

Replete) the night dissolved, but in the light,
A grey-eyed light, under the draining hills
Some pools of woodland remained and in them owls
And beside my sleepwalking, along the borders

Owls accompanied me, they were echoing
From wood to wood, into the hesitant day
I carried the owls in their surviving wells
Of night-time. The fittest are a fatal breed.

They'd do without sleep if they possibly could
And meter it for the rest of us. I like
Humans who harbour the dark in their open
Eyes all day. They seem more kin, more kind. They are

The ones not listening while the ruling voices
Further impair our hearing. They are away
With the owls, they ride the dreaming hooting hills
Down, down, into an infinite pacific.

David Constantine

The Wasps

The apples on the tree are full of wasps;
Red apples, racing like hearts. The summer pushes
Her tongue into the winter's throat.

But at six today, like rain, like the first drops,
The wasps came battering softly at the black glass.
They want the light, the cold is at their backs.

That morning last year when the light had been left on
The strange room terrified the heart in me,
I could not place myself, didn't know my own

Insect scribble: then saw the whole soft
Pelt of wasps, its underbelly, the long black pane
Yellow with visitants, it seethed, the glass sounded.

I bless my life: that so much wants in.

David Constantine

The Ecology of Love

Mankind, the spirit of the earth, the synthesis
of individuals and peoples, the paradoxical
conciliation of the element with the whole, and
of unity with multitude—all these are called
Utopian and yet they are biologically necessary.
And for them to be incarnated in the world all
we may well need is to imagine our power of
loving developing until it embraces all of
human life as well as the earth.

Teilhard de Chardin

Little Cosmic Dust Poem

Out of the debris of dying stars,
this rain of particles
that waters the waste with brightness . . .

The sea-wave of atoms hurrying home,
collapse of the giant,
unstable guest who cannot stay . . .

The sun's heart reddens and expands,
his mighty aspiration is lasting,
as the shell of his substance
one day will be white with frost.

In the radiant field of Orion
great hordes of stars are forming,
just as we see every night,
fiery and faithful to the end.

Out of cold and fleeing dust
that is never and always,
the silence and waste to come . . .

This arm, this hand,
my voice, your face, this love.

John Haines

Amo Ergo Sum

Because I love
      The sun pours out its rays of living gold
      Pours out its gold and silver on the sea.

Because I love
      The earth upon her astral spindle winds
      Her ecstasy-producing dance.

Because I love
      Clouds travel on the winds through wide skies,
      Skies wide and beautiful, blue and deep.

Because I love
>Wind blows white sails,
>The wind blows over flowers, the sweet wind blows.

Because I love
>The ferns grow green, and green the grass, and green
>The transparent sunlit trees.

Because I love
>Larks rise up from the grass
>And all the leaves are full of singing birds.

Because I love
>The summer air quivers with a thousand wings,
>Myriads of jewelled eyes burn in the light.

Because I love
>The iridescent shells upon the sand
>Take forms as fine and intricate as thought.

Because I love
>There is an invisible way across the sky,
>Birds travel by that way, the sun and moon
>And all the stars travel that path by night.

Because I love
>There is a river flowing all night long.

Because I love
>All night the river flows into my sleep,
>Ten thousand living things are sleeping in my arms,
>And sleeping wake, and flowing are at rest.

Kathleen Raine

Love-song

He has lived with her tribe, become fluent
in her language, trading rhythms,
textures of subtle form.

Each day they dance colours, shape forces.
A silent mage, he draws back her veil:
honours the beauty of imperfection.

Joan Poulson

Beginning

Doing nothing about this,
Or the day, or the time.
I don't know and I don't know
Lying back with the light behind my eyes
Watching the mind stop—
Watching my watch stop.
Letting it all stop,
Letting it go.

Thought-free, as the light is
As I drop whatever words come, one by one
Into the light's depth, the lap lap of the water
And a half buried book left open in the sand
With its torn bleached pages I saw myself
Slowly scattering into the water—
And pages and pages I just crossed out.
Standing in the water and the water was light
Splashing it over each other and laughing
As we talked to each other with our eyes—

And now you lie with your face in silence,
I look at myself dissolving as I step
Forward to where I can carry nothing
Only the light of what already is in me,
Becoming that self as it has always been
Endlessly begun, and about to begin.

Jay Ramsay

Of Grass

It was the shade of grass—no, something greener
We touched on shortly before sleep, so soft, so bright,
No metaphor could touch or scumble it,
I cannot speak it though my mouth is green.

In a dream following a cobra nestled
Against my chest—we wrestled as in play
Then I lay poisoned in the open air,
I was nothing and the grass was nothing,

Only my fingers were aware and moved
In search of feeling, but they found
Nothing except a tongue and it was yours

Speaking of something in a foreign language
And I being your tongue's interpreter
Understood the word you spoke as grass.

George Szirtes

Sprigs of Rosemary

I bring this sprig of rosemary; but what is rosemary for?
It is for releasing memory, for increasing memory's store.

Yet few memories come back; childhood oppresses
With its weight of sullen fears. My life regresses

Into the black. I cannot remember what I said or did.
A haphazard crow flies at an angle to the wood.

So many memories gone into the gap under the falling wave,
Ash to the metallic fire, the blankness of the grave.

There's a paradox here. I pluck rosemary to mark what's absent,
To acknowledge what is over with aromatic scent,

To let it go with grace—and then I remember images of you,
The lapis lazuli against the whiteness of your neck, your sigh

At the eternal candour of its blue. You are the one somewhere
In my imagination with sprigs of rosemary in her hair

And sprays of bay leaves in her hands, whose radiant eyes
Bring back, at memory's furthest root, the glint of Paradise.

Peter Abbs

Chrysanths

These then for you:
tough flowers
whose stems are stalks
wiry yet brittle
rather trees than plants
leaves like alarmed acanthus
as if the oak had seen a ghost
and aromatic
as a bunch of herbs.
Rubbed
their scent takes off your head
oily like mint
or eucalyptus
but dry with dusts of sage
wild thyme
and the prickly snuff
of rosemary.
They've come into bloom
reluctantly
holding their petals in
like burned fingers.
I've got them to open
only by looking
so hard at them.
At last
drawn to respond
they've disgorged
gold-mines.
Their spectrum's
sacrificial:
the light's not split
but pressed
till it bleeds suns.
In Japan
they are a badge of lovers
who, rather than divide,
in their embrace
die blinded.

Donald Atkinson

Russet Apples

Lie back against the pillows:
and again, as if for the first time,
I give you a russet apple.

In our country the custom
is love first, and then apples:
a ritual celebration
of our unhoped-for return
after aeons of wandering where
there was nobody, or the next best thing—

some lover who didn't care
enough to let it be right;
some man who wouldn't trust,
some women who didn't dare;
where always she was hiding a hate,
or he had to fondle an image
to help him get it on.

Now we've passed the gate,
the land is ours again
and the apple's into the secret;
feel how it loves us as you bite
and the juice comes, cider-sweet,
leaf-sour, and the rusty bronze skin
gleams wet in candle-light,

and feel when I kiss you how
within the mouth's dark space
there is no I or you
but only a fragrance of endless
orchards that waited here, always
ripening, longing to welcome us
back into paradise.

Grevel Lindop

Appletree

You turn and sigh,
tugging the sheet, and I'm
plucked from my reverie.

Five a.m. and the rain
pelting the windows.
I settle again,

retrace my steps. It's
still where it was, arched
above the blanched grasses, fruits

glowing in sunlight, relic
of an abandoned garden. We
push through the thick

undergrowth, climbing the slope
until we stand in the shadow
of its branches. You stretch up

and forward, your print skirt lifting
behind your knees. The apple
is in your hand. Here nothing

has changed. You extend your arm.
My mouth is open, the white
flesh sweet and warm.

Jem Poster

Between Voyages

You brought me a seahorse, succulent shells.
The boat in the garden nudges the hedge;
its shrouds call up storms and a distant sea
where people, like sails, flap impatiently
with the pain of the land-bound watching tides.

Rain skitters down tiles: the gutters have gone.
Water flows below floors, rises up through
the ground floating spring bulbs and snails; their shells
striped whorls, brittle as memories of your voice —
close as the cold day, dark as our lost north.

I savour the sea horse, stroke a starfish
I once found — stiff-fingered in the sea coal
of a wintered town. All day, through the house,
I have shells beneath my feet. The floors give
and flood, gulls wheel above this inland roof.

Robyn Bolam

Divers

We knew infallibly: love marked the spot.
Oh, charted faces, time-worn and marine!

After a year tossed among waves of hair,
Brimmed eyes and flotsam glances,

In a free fall, we leave the surface play
And work of light; traverse the permeable deeps

That close about our origins. All births
Are dumbly recognized in these slow worlds

Where silence and the beautiful darknesses
Drift and brood above the spirit's dancing floor.

In echoing cadences of green slow-motion,
We celebrate the ancient mysteries:

Combers for lost gold in a lodge of sand,
Amazed discoverers of our buried selves.

Peter Scupham

At Cuckmere Estuary

We stand on the shingle as night comes in. Behind us
Storm clouds, bruised and red, slump to the Downs. This is
The last violence of the haemorrhaging sun. Lightning forks

And flickers vertical at the edge. All that our eclectic times
Have claimed dissolves. We listen to a silence whose signs
Are hard and hazardous to read. We are novices. New-comers.

Inland a siren wails and spreads its shrill alarm. At last
The stillness returns more intensely reticent for the dissonance.
The reason is . . . The reason is . . . There are no reasons left:

Platitudes jostle in the gaps. The healing word takes flight
In the daily battle-ground of microphones and hype
And singing Orpheus drowns in a flood of camera light.

We close our eyes and sense the breeze against our flesh.
The salt burns our mouths. There's no desire to talk. We drink
In the forgotten dark. The tide spumes white against the chalk.

Peter Abbs

Kingfisher

December took us where the idling water
Rose in a ghost of smoke, its banks hard-thatched
With blanching reeds, the sun in a far quarter.

Short days had struck a bitter chain together
In links of blue and white so closely matched
They made an equipoise we called the weather.

There, the first snowfall grew to carapace,
The pulse beneath it beating slow and blind,
And every kind of absence marked the face

On which we walked as if we were not lost,
As if there was a something there to find
Beneath a sleep of branches grey with frost.

We smiled, and spoke small words which had no hold
Upon the darkness we had carried there,
Our bents and winter dead-things, wisps of cold.

And then, from wastes of stub and nothing came
The Kingfisher, whose instancy laid bare
His proof that ice and sapphire conjure flame.

Peter Scupham

Totems

As if retrieving pebbles
 filmed with shine
from the curved spine of a beach,
 waves lisping
our faces stung with salt, our
 talk fresh with
discovery, we carried
 each season
to our door: catkins, first snow
 of blossom,
the flotsam of our journeys,
 sweet chestnuts'
porcupines, pectorals of
 cones. Turning
varied textures in our hands,
 fleetingly
touched by their strangeness, subtly
 changed. Bringing
the outside in, so the house
 swam in its
wider rhythms, the flow of
 storm-clouds, hills,
moraine, the shuttling arc
 of the sun.

Lynne Elson

Love Poem

It was the Kingfisher I saw there first—
a blue-blink in the ghyll. Then the hazel—hung
with yellow kitten-tongues.

That day we summoned sun, our friendship
sang. We walked—and talked about our lives—
our separate skies.

Climbing up—through Ruskin's garden—I smiled—
and caught the smile returned—
behind your eyes a child's warmth burned.

From time to time the grassy route
gave way—to wild scents—freed
by our play. And then we were besieged

by tiredness—caught the steam-boat
from the deck—ran fast through rocks—
and jumped the rope. There we were afloat

sailing over to the northern shore.
I saw the skies grow heavy—and descend.
Felt the pelting evening storm hitting land.

Judith Galloway

Rainbow

firebreathing
I let you lead me
      up the burnt hill and the gorse
          beside the stream

              my heart bursts
                a heathermix of love and
                    fear and feathers

                    from that perfect hoop
                    an arrow
              a bow of rain
            over the brown and purple sea

         my skin is melting
     reforming
scaling off
I am the dragon I am afraid of

                    Carolyn Finlay

Peacock

A man's fist may be very gentle
When he takes a butterfly off the pane
And feels the tickle of her wings like desperate eyes.

She seemed to know what she wanted.
Bodily she made the sign of it against the glass,
Sign of her need, sign of the impediment.

October again. The wind.
The trees gasp and are suddenly naked
And everything whirled in the air is dead or dying.

She had opened like an illumination
Under the wall-lamp above their pillow
Still as a brooch, and the savage wind at the pane.

Eyes in the dark. The man has her in his head.

                    David Constantine

The Snowing Globe

A trick of the fingers
And the world turns.
A drift of tiny snow.

The frosted reindeer,
Lost in a Christmas wood—
They will make room for us.

Thicker, colder than airs.
Softly, neatly,
You hurry to where I wait.

Your rough black coat
Brushes the sidling flakes.
They cling like burrs.

Under an ancient light,
Snow in your dark hair
Dissolves; glistens like tears.

Our eyes take fire.
We are preserved in amber
These fourteen crystal years.

Somewhere, our unborn children
Smile with your smile.
The snow is settling now.

Peter Scupham

Bedrock

for Masa

Snowmelt pond,   warm granite
we make camp,
no thought of finding more.
and nap
and leave our minds to the wind.

on the bedrock, gently tilting,
sky and stone,

teach me to be tender.

the touch that nearly misses —
brush of glances —
tiny steps —
that finally cover worlds
        of hard terrain.
cloud wisps and mists
gathered into slate blue
bolts of summer rain.

tea together in the purple starry eve;
new moon soon to set,
why does it take so
long to learn to
love,
        we laugh
                and grieve.

Gary Snyder

Saying Something

saying nothing
saying something
saying it
and the light bright on it
like the afterimage of a straight road

saying nothing
saying something
walking
down the street
with the river
being understood and a feeling
a good feeling
of how it feels under the houses
how the red brick
by the river
feels
and saying it

we keep on
saying nothing
saying something
saying it
not saying it
I can't believe we keep on
saying it not saying it
and all the time the door
half open
and the light
on the garden
beautiful
and you
beautiful
saying it and not
and all the time the light lying
all over the garden
and us

Carolyn Finlay

Aubade

Light as a rose
he sleeps beside
his first cradle,

intent on stillness
but breathing firmly
as if breath would always

when the time comes.
But for now he will keep
his excellent secrets

— the glossy function
of heart and lungs,
arms and legs,

the legend of his mouth.
His voice sleeps,
his sex sleeps.

In the faint shine
of morning, when
flesh can be chilled

I draw up the sheet
and cover him
to save us both.

Carol Rumens

Mother and Daughter by the North Sea

I watch you walk through your grief,
ease from the husk of your inland house

into salt light. We hear the sea's lisp,
a whisper of ebb on the out-breath

and watch a crab shake castanets
and run its red world sideways.

The sands are blue with reflected sky
by cliffs as soft as creamed almonds.

Shell of your shell, I feel the pull
of bright water. Gems roll at our feet,

capsules of fire in the ash of our hands.
Cornelian, amber, chalcedony,

fragments from Scotland and Norway,
atoms of self. My love for you

is littoral: I want to net each stone
for your house, each moment

burnished by the sea, as you tread
the beach in your old brown shoes

and the Norfolk sky breathes round you,
the sun holding its celandine to your face.

Lynne Wycherley

Three Sisters

Three sisters, like three hens, eye one another;
six hands, like sparrows, flutter up and down
making wreaths for you, the sister's brother,
from winter flowers whose petals have turned brown,
from rosemary and basil's grey and blue,
from lavender, and ivy from the apple;
from snowdrops tied in ribbon, berried yew —
six hands like hymns; the kitchen like a chapel
where hens and rabbits wander in and out,
and flowers and fruit trees grow between the stones:
three lemons for the mousse; a lily; trout,
ten tickling fingers checking it for bones.
Chop, chop. That's it. There's nothing we can do.
A fly. A knife. The sickly smell of rue.

Selima Hill

Planting a Sequoia

All afternoon my brothers and I have worked in the
      orchard,
Digging this hole, laying you into it, carefully packing
      the soil.
Rain blackened the horizon, but cold winds kept it
      over the Pacific,
And the sky above us stayed the dull gray
Of an old year coming to an end.

In Sicily a father plants a tree to celebrate his first
      son's birth —
An olive or a fig tree — a sign that the earth has once
      more life to bear.
I would have done the same, proudly laying new
      stock into my father's orchard.
A green sapling rising among the twisted apple
      boughs.
A promise of new fruit in other autumns.

But today we kneel in the cold planting you, our
      native giant,
Defying the practical custom of our fathers,
Wrapping in your roots a lock of hair, a piece of an
      infant's birth cord,
All that remains above earth of a first-born son.
A few stray atoms brought back to the elements.

We will give you what we can — our labour and our
      soil,
Water drawn from the earth when the skies fail.
Nights scented with the ocean fog, days softened by
      the circuit of bees.
We plant you in the corner of the grove, bathed in
      western light,
A slender shoot against the sunset.

And when our family is no more, all of his unborn
      brothers dead,
Every niece and nephew scattered, the house torn
      down,
His mother's beauty ashes in the air,
I want you to stand among strangers, all young and
      ephemeral to you,
Silently keeping the secret of your birth.

Dana Gioia

Grandfather in the Garden

Digging was always my worst work.
After ten minutes I would blow
My scalding hands and watch him fork
Quite effortlessly the rain-heavy clay
Of a new garden, meticulous and slow
Labour that soon tired a boy.

All his life a cultivator
Of the soil's best things, ingenious
Exterminator of what opposed his sure
Design. Summers wet or dry found him
Aware of deep conspiracies of earth
To damage or destroy the year's triumph.

Thus he squared his jaw, donned ancient
Clothes, and set to digging out his
Fear. Late evenings I'd be sent
To call him in, a dark and elemental
Shape by then, the ruins of a young man's face
Still visible behind the years, the toil.

A labourer and architect,
He taught patience in slow lessons
And one man's dedication to a craft.
From his cracked hands I watched the brittle seed
Cast surely for the future, the unborn;
Those acts of affirmation his deep need.

Robert Minhinnick

Words for Some Ash

Poor parched man, we had to squeeze
Dental sponge against your teeth,
So that moisture by degrees
Dribbled to the mouth beneath.

Christmas Day your pupils crossed,
Staring at your nose's tip,
Seeking there the air you lost
Yet still gaped for, dry of lip.

Now you are a bag of ash
Scattered on a coastal ridge,
Where you watched the distant crash,
Ocean on a broken edge.

Death has wiped away each sense;
Fire took muscle, bone, and brains;
Next may rain leach discontents
From your dust, wash what remains

Deeper into damper ground
Till the granules work their way
Down to unseen streams, and bound
Briskly in the water's play;

May you lastly reach the shore,
Joining tide without intent,
Only worried any more
By the currents' argument

Thom Gunn

Weaving the
Symbolic Web

*No longer in a merely physical universe,
man lives in a symbolic universe. Language,
myth, art, and religion are parts of this
universe. They are the varied threads which
weave the symbolic net, the tangled web
of human experience.*

Ernst Cassirer

Ice Man

You seem tenuous and brittle as a dry
Stick insect
But even after five thousand years
Your sinews
Hold you obstinately together.

So much you have to teach us. Just
Being there
You turn our arrogant nomenclature
Of time
Upside down. You can't be clutching your
Copper axe;
But, foolishly, we see you are.

You humble us with your grasp
And use
Of eighteen different kinds of wood;
The way
You took grass, sinew, feather, flint
And bark,
Threading them into your confident life.

You tease us:
Lying down where our borders disappear;
So both
Austria and Italy argued you their own.

They nearly
Rent you down the middle to be fair.
We sift
Your every crevice, sieve your secrets;

Finding even
What you had for your final meal; where
You lived;
What your nails had lately worked upon.

You are
Our countryman and brother, come to ask
Why we
In five thousand years between, and despite

The lives
Of prophets, sages, Gautama and Christ,

Have learned
To love less ourselves, our world and each other.
We muster
Information, detailed information
In answer.
But we cannot penetrate your silence.

You tell us
We are tiny in the immensity of ice.

Michael Woodward

A Hymn to Demeter

Pardon us
that we will
our end & forgive

the poet
his ambition
to stand alone

on a high peak
surveying
the waste.

Take the map
from our hands
which we take
for the world

& let us be
where earth
and waters meet

& make, for you,
a song.

Jeremy Hooker

An Invocation to Pan

Come, eye of the forest
come, beast-footed
stag-crowned
man-membered; come, tree-sinewed
soil-rubbed, leaf-garlanded;
come, goat-nimble
come, bird-joyful
come, fox-cunning;
out of the boles and burrows
out of the humps and hollows
out of the heaps of leaves
out of mist and darkness
out of sunshafts, gold motes,
flowers, insects humming:
brown lying down in summer by the river
your flute notes cool
and black striding up from the woods in winter
wreathed in fogs, your voice belling;
come, old one, come, green one,
tree-protector, beast-befriender
good shepherd, wise steward:
come, earth-brother
long long lost
long long lost
let us find you
call you
call you up, out, back, forth—
be here now!
O musk of fur sour
in the wind, your branched head
through the thickets
coming, coming
in your power, your power, your power.

Hilary Llewellyn-Williams

Song of Orpheus

I was the first in an unforgettable line.
Honoured. Then maligned. Inventor of the lyre.
Who failed Eurydice. Who raided the archives

Of the body. Found sex. Found death. Who from guilt
Made beauty. A lyric on the blood-soaked tongue.
Tested by fire, cleansed by water, absolved by it.

Who plucking the taut gut
Drew gulls. Drew rocks. Drew stones. Drew trees
Lumbering to the one bright edge. Who stalked

The labyrinth of bone. Who staggered through the hall
Of skulls. Who came back. Little to show:
Stark line, staccato sound, a broken cadence.

Who outsang the sirens,
Copywriters, entertainers, impresarios of a jaded time.
Whose one law is transformation.

Whose one rule is song. Who floats bleeding battered
On the tidal stream. A singing head
To calm the dizzy stars. Slow their cooling.

Peter Abbs

Orpheus Attending

for A.L. Lloyd. collector of folk song

Always between the tracks your singular voice,
recording angel: tremulous, alert,
a low-pitched flute, but syllabled by water-
over-stones, long days in Maramures.
Wrung from a dissonance of grief and laughter,
compounded of all ages and both sex,
a spoken counter-tenor trapped in the throat
of all our mothers, full of milk and song,
its words came gentle as Gielgud on the tongue
but salt with transatlantic, the Celtic vowels
haunted by Appalachian cadences.
Wenceslaus-treading in the steps of Bartok,
ear keened to the earth through the feet,
you taped for the ends of time those wauling cries
that birthed and deathed our ancestors.
Sounds to screw the gut or race the heart-beat.
Work-songs from Eboli, hot dust on the notes.
Balkan kalendi sung for the plain girl
who dies unmarried, her wedding beyond death
to the axed pine, prettied with rosettes,
they plant as an after-lover on her grave
to keep happy her ghost in the cold nights.
To those villagers, song was the soul dreaming
Or the pained cry of the deed as it flew
from the strings of the heart. A matrix for
journeys, places. Song was society
nor were we out of it. Ritualled by that,
we caught the earth's pulse and measured time
with flinty rocks, birds, snakes, domestic beasts,
and all the choreograph of trees that danced in Ovid.
Proleptic link man, kinder Tiresias, you—
foreseeing the uncommuned dearth we're aimed at—
stored up against a time of desperate new beginnings
all that miraculous circumstance of song
for folk to feed on. Grant when the last bough breaks
your tapes play philomel beyond our earth-crimes.

Donald Atkinson

Persephone

I

I see as through a skylight in my brain
The mole strew its buildings in the rain,

The swallows turn above their broken home
And all my acres in delirium.

II

Straitjacketed by cold and numskulled
Now sleep the welladjusted and the skilled—

The bat folds its wing like a winter leaf,
The squirrel in its hollow holds aloof.

III

The weasel and ferret, the stoat and fox
Move hand in glove across the equinox.

I can tell how softly their footsteps go—
Their footsteps borrow silence from the snow.

Michael Longley

Bran's Song

I saw a realm of blood and fire,
a blistered field,
a butchered horse,
a broken man returned from war
to a wife's silence,
a mother's curse.

Above that fallen realm: a hill,
a granite tump,
a grassy knoll,
a thorny groin of earth and stone
warming its flanks
beneath the sun.

Beneath that hump: a cave of rock,
a darkened hollow
in the hill,
a dry and rough-hewn vault of night,
a womb of dust,
starless and still.

Inside that cave I saw a head,
a severed head
of high degree,
whose liquid eye was fixed upon
some trackless realm
I could not see.

I took the head between my hands,
I shook it hard,
I shouted: "Wake!
What ails you that you do not watch
this world that suffers
for your sake?"

"I am awake! Your broken world
allows the light
into my eye,
within this place where realm meets realm
I watch each nation
thrive and die.

And then, beyond your broken world,
I watch the truth
that waits behind:
The blazing tree of leaf and flame
where joy and sorrow
intertwine.

Between my hands the head was dust,
the cave had closed
and disappeared,
through fields of wheat a horseman rode
to a wife's embrace,
a mother's tears.

Hugh Lupton

Xochiquetzal

The firefighters of Chernobyl
lie naked
on sloping beds
in sterile rooms,
without eyelashes
or salivary glands

o death
take them lightly
as the Colombian goddess
who makes love
to young warriors
on the battlefield

holding a butterfly
between her lips.

Pauline Stainer

Mary Magdalene

I was watching Miriam
abandon herself to Jesus.

I saw her pour alabaster oil
gently over his head.

Her frenzied hands
caress his face.

Her long wisps of ebony hair
brush over his feet,

drying the great outpouring
of his tears.

I watched him curl
his fingers around hers,

lift her head
from his knees.

Stroke her cheek.

Drink her love
into holy week.

Lucy Calcott

Adulteress

I see him
Drawing in the sand,
The girl glancing up at him.

I see all of us
Standing around,
With that quick-to-judge

Look in our eyes.
I turn from the noise,
To the silence

To find him again.
Gnarled feet.
Scarred hands.

Long piano-playing fingers
Drawing
In the sand.

Lucy Calcott

Canute

(c.994–1035)

No monument for me   but the beach;
today I risked it all   today I told them
no, I showed them   the meaning of all-mighty.

I was sick of their fawning   their falling flat at my feet
so I took them   treading over stones
steered them across the sand   to the sea-gulls' field;

laughed as I made them drag   and lift my throne
past the high flood mark   to the whale's pathway;
loved the licks of spray   the whipping of the wind.

The weather was wild   the sky thick and low
my blood was beating   like the blackening waves
and I knew, no question,   from that knife-edge moment

I would have immortality   not from glorious martyrdom
but from looking like a fool.   The sea-fowl's screech,
a mockery of laughing,   lifted and looped over the water;

the water lifted stones   stones stirred the sand
sand slipped under water.   Faces of fools
gaped at the grey flood   gawked at a king

whose ship had sailed   from his mind-shore.
No monument for me now   but the sea
stubborn against my stand   and the eternal tide

the running-track of ships   pushing as it should
thundering past all of us   God's great poem
pounding on the shifting ground   of misunderstanding.

Josephine Abbott

On Piero della Francesca's 'Magdalen'
(from Attraction)

The brow is proud, and though the eyes are inward,
The mouth is a voluptuous eruption;
Her hair is loose, for mourning or for love.

She was the first to see the risen Christ,
     a courtesan,
The woman once possessed by seven devils;
       here upright, stable,
Substantial as a tablet of the Law.

Piero dresses her in billow green,
     or the green
   of a serpent, but drawn
Virginal by white at waist and wrist,
      all simplicity,
    columnar, calm
Within the slow explosion of her cloak —
   its red skin, its white flesh broken,
     the blast
    of Eve's shattered apple
  that made an open book
   of good and evil,
and slammed shut Eden,
   a single infraction
making law of rupture and attraction.

       Martin Schmandt

The Isenheim Altar of Matthias Grünewald

The lamb is come down: from the cross, the cross folded forever
in its forelimb. It is open-eyed, slain of course, alive, blood still
draining to the cup, to the end of time; head love-tilted, eyes ever
fastened on its own conquest, an ear for its long-beheaded Baptist,
itself the heart-bleeder, the way-changer, the only true rememberer,
sage innocent: exemplar. Who knew to join these two: little lamb
with swollen, ripped and pitted Death? It was Matthias the time-tearer.
This is his bold oblation, presentation, communion with the saints,
Augustine, Sebastian, Mary, Jerome, John, Anthony: *therapeuticum*,
five centuries old, for the sicknesses of sin; *heiltum*, healing agent
still, this suffering for ours, our wounds, whose staunching, salving, is
perpetually sustained by this issue, of blood, the cup, the lamb, its cross.

Frances Howarth

Brueghel's Snow

Here in the snow:
three hunters with dogs and pikes
trekking over a hill,
into and out of those famous footprints—
famous and still.

What did they catch?
They have little to show
on their bowed backs.
Unlike the delicate skaters below,
these are grim; they look ill.

In the village, it's zero.
Bent shapes in black clouts,
raw faces aglow
in the firelight, burning the wind
for warmth, or their hunger's kill.

What happens next?
In the unpainted picture?
The hunters arrive, pull
off their caked boots, curse the weather
slump down over stoups . . .

Who's painting them now?
What has survived to unbandage
my eyes as I trudge through this snow,
with my dog and stick,
four hundred winters ago?

Anne Stevenson

A Woman Pouring Milk

Thank you Vermeer
for a glimpse of interiors
and a door that opens
into rooms beyond rooms
where a brown light falls

And your Woman Pouring Milk
cares nothing for this
fame you've laid on her
yellow and blue
but she *is* famous
You've caught
what's famous about her

The jug   how
tenderly she holds it

And why shouldn't I
be content that way
with how the light
grazes my shoulder

Yes but his woman's
not even aware
of her own contentment
and I in trying to be so
am always at one remove

Even if I shouted
she would not turn
towards the thought
that she's a beauty looked at

There is bread on her table
and her hands are bread
and her face is bread
and I wish I was bread
and not this thinking thing
always at one remove

I want to be poured
the way she pours herself
out into the mixture.

Paul Matthews

Caliban's Books

Hair oil, boiled sweets, chalk dust, squid's ink . . .
Bear with me. I'm trying to conjure my father,
age fourteen, as Caliban — picked by Mr Quinn
for the role he was born to play because
'I was the handsomest boy at school'
he'll say, straight-faced, at fifty.
This isn't easy. I've only half the spell,
and I won't be born for twenty years.
I'm trying for rainlight on Belfast Lough
and listening for a small, blunt accent
barking over the hiss of a stove getting louder like surf.
But how can I read when the schoolroom's gone
black as the hold of a ship? Start again.

Hair oil, boiled sweets . . .
But his paperbacks are crumbling in my hands,
seachanged bouquets, each brown page
scribbled on, underlined, memorized,
forgotten like used pornography:
The Pocket Treasury of English Verse,
How to Win Friends and Influence People,
Thirty Days To a More Powerful Vocabulary.

Fish stink, pitch stink, seaspray, cedarwood . . .
I seem to have brought us to the port of Naples,
midnight, to a shadow below deck
dreaming of a distant island.
So many years, so many ports ago!
The moment comes. It slips from the hold
and knucklewalks across the dark piazza
sobbing *maestro! maestro!* But the duke's long dead
and all his magic books are drowned.

Michael Donaghy

Descartes and the Stove

Thrusting its armoury of hot delight,
    Its negroid belly at him, how the whole
Contraption threatened to melt him
    Into recognition. Outside, the snow
Starkened all that snow was not—
    The boughs' nerve-net, angles and gables
Denting the brilliant hoods of it. The foot-print
    He had left on entering, had turned
To a firm dull gloss, and the chill
    Lined it with a fur of frost. Now
The last blaze of day was changing
    All white to yellow, filling
With bluish shade the slots and spoors
    Where, once again, badger and fox would wind
Through the phosphorescence. All leaned
    Into that frigid burning, corded tight
By the lightlines as the slow sun drew
    Away and down. The shadow, now,
Defined no longer: it filled, then overflowed
    Each fault in snow, dragged everything
Into its own anonymity of blue
    Becoming black. The great mind
Sat with his back to the unreasoning wind
    And doubted, doubted at his ear
The patter of ash and, beyond, the snow-bound farms,
    Flora of flame and iron contingency
And the moist reciprocation of his palms.

Charles Tomlinson

The Incomprehensible Ingredients of Fire

Dear Christopher Smart,

I saw on the map today that Shipbourne where you were born is on the Medway, downstream from where I live in Forest Row. It pleases me to think so. You are dead—I know that. But it's the same river. Why should a simple thing like death keep us from talking?

William Blake called this valley *Beulah*—a soft dreamy place. Impossible to stay here. Maybe even as a child you heard your madness whistling from the thornbrakes. Something beckoning.

Oh I've read how you won those poetry prizes at Cambridge. You could have made quite a career for yourself I suppose, except that you read God's name *in the grain of wood, . . . in the incomprehensible ingredients of fire,* and had to go down on your knees in the presence of it.

They locked you away for that, but could not keep you from your *Jubilate*.

I've been reading that 'mad' poem of yours again. Don't think me just another of those gawpers you complain of. It's true I don't understand it, but I could read whole libraries of books, understand them, and never come to poetry.

But in your book I find the very incomprehensible ingredients of fire you spoke of. All comprehending falls away before this kindling. I mean my eyes look out of the window differently knowing that Sun and Moon are secretly at work there *weaving a garment for us*.

It was a shirt of fire they wove you. How can a man live whose eyes see nothing but the Glory?

Paul Matthews

John Clare's Madness

Northamptonshire's
deadly flat
spreads beneath the hawk.

Watching hedgerows
and the muddy lanes.
Sharp eyed for winter he's aware again

how each small movement's plain
to the eye awake
for food or touch of rain

to make his feathers start.
My pen touched paper
just the same. Alert to follow

exactly what I saw. Said
exactly how I speak.
Now,

Northborough's
fields hold nothing
— my house an empty shell.

Above Helpstone
the hawk circles
the house that I have failed.

There is a small body
caught in his claws,
it cries to the hawk in fear.

I said, beat, beat, strange wings,
what is won then lost
comes back with the fiercest pain.

David Whyte

Hölderlin

for Paul Hoffmann

The river remembers,
then crumples in a frown of loss:
a garden of children and laundry at the brink,
the white face of a man shut in the mind's tall tower.

In the October garden, where the carpenter's children
played between the high wall and the water,
apples fall, and fire-tongues of cherry
crackle in the grass for us to shuffle.

The great willow that the poet knew,
only half itself since the hurricane,
kneels into a current that's deeper
and more powerful than it seems.

Upstairs, in his white, three-windowed hemisphere,
where for forty years they cared for him, light
shivers on the ceiling, bird-shadows touch and go,
things that were clear break up and flow away:

his poems on the wall,
quick freehand in the visitors' book,
a jar of flowers on bare boards,
a drift of red leaves on three windowsills.

So small, his bed must have been here,
his table there for the light, and the door
where the carpenter's daughter listened for his rages
and brought him bread, meat, a bowl of milk.

The swan turns on her own reflection. Silence
is her image. Currents pull. The willow
trawls its shadow, searching for something
in the broken face of water.

Gillian Clarke

Turner's Seas

We call them beautiful
Turner's appalling seas, shipwreck and deluge
Where man's contraptions, mast and hull,
Lurch, capsize, shatter to driftwood in the whelming surge and swell,
Men and women like spindrift hurled in spray
And no survivors in those sliding glassy graves.
Doomed seafarers on unfathomed waters,
We yet call beautiful those gleaming gulphs that break in foam,
Beautiful the storm-foreboding skies, the lurid west,
Beautiful the white radiance that dissolves all.
What recognition from what deep source cries
Glory to the universal light that walks the ever-running waves,
What memory deeper than fear, what recollection of untrammelled joy
Our scattered falling drops retain of gleaming ocean's unending play?

Kathleen Raine

Turner is Lashed to the Mast

I did not paint it to be understood
but to show how water
makes the wind visible,
how the sea strikes
like a steel gauntlet

I scent the blizzard
lashed like Odysseus,
the air laced with diamond,
salt-pearl at my wrist

indistinctness is my forte
a gauze backdrop,
a ship hulling
to the hiss
of the vortex

I would fix
such sirens,
before unseen currents
disperse their dissolve.

Pauline Stainer

Darwin in Patagonia

I brood on the process
of perfection and the less
perfectly gliding squirrels

in the parallel light of the afternoons
I study the creatures
constructed for twilight

I am never completely well;
the lakes hang like mica templates
in the brackish air

the winds pour from La Plata,
flies breed in the navels
of young mammals

I record the diving thrushes,
the woodpeckers
in the treeless wastes

the ice floes
which may formerly
have transported foxes;

across the straits
the barbarians multiply
The horse among the trumpets saith 'Aha!'

I take quinine and speculate
on the slashing claw
in the folded schists

but still dream
of Adam naming
the doubtful species

and wake shuddering
at the irreproachable design
of the eye.

Pauline Stainer

Homage to Paul Celan

Something will be, later
that fills up with you
and lifts itself
to a mouth
—from *Zeitgehoft*

Still, as it always is
'After you'

To an edge that no one
Has surpassed—

And a voice
We must never learn to repress

Speaking as it does
(whether you like it or not . . .)

In the syntax
Of its singular irregular integrity

Where the birds sing
In the wine of the dawn air
Throat-liquefying in counterpoint
Over the listening oasis of the garden

Above, beyond, within
The river of grief you drowned in

The Seine-Sane Insensate Asylum
Shadow-stained over Everywhere

Where you live on
                              in our inner ear

Jay Ramsay

Ars Poetica

It will listen to the arias of whales.
It will wake to the dawn yelp of the gull.
It will affirm the blue canticle of the skylark, the black croak of the frog.
It will be schooled by the sibilance of water, be attuned to the hard
consonance of rock.
It will gut dictionaries.
It will eat etymologies.
It will eavesdrop on the spontaneous ramblings of children.
It will tour fairgrounds with a microphone.
It will tremble before the glance of Beauty.
It will taste the white vinegar of death.
It will honour silence.
It will be a crucible open to stars and dust.
It will expound the laws of Quantum Mechanics and recite the Proverbs of
Blake.
It will aspire to the levity of the butterfly crossing nuclear zones.
It will be born in blood, rise in estrangement, climax in breath.
It will remain in quest.

Peter Abbs

Loaves and Fishes

This is not
the age of information.

This is *not*
the age of information.

Forget the news,
and the radio,
and the blurred screen.

This is the time
of loaves
and fishes.

People are hungry,
and one good word is bread
for a thousand.

David Whyte

The Thin End of the Wedge

There was no way forward.
There was no way back.
I sat at my desk
With nothing but time

Ticking on my wrist-watch.
Into the blankness
Came a thought
Like the toe of a stranger

In a long-unvisited house.
'What do you want?' I said,
Expecting no solace
From such an intruder.

'I am the wedge,' the thought informed me,
'Driving into your brain.
You will feel nothing at first,
But slowly you will see

Time split apart, the past and the future
No longer relevant, as the
Ticking of your watch becomes
Geared to the nucleus.'

I was not amused,
Until the thought
Drove into me, all the way home.
'What now?' I laughed,

Creation all around me
An imminent possibility only.
'Shall I create the world?
Or shall I let it

Remain uncreated?' I heard
The question clearly enough,
As the thought withdrew from my head
Like an axe of light.

Sebastian Barker

Sabbaths

After the slavery of the body, dumbfoundment
of the living flesh in the order of spending
and wasting, then comes the enslavement
of consciousness, the incarnation of mind
in machines. Once the mind is reduced
to the brain, then it falls within the grasp
of the machine. It is the mind incarnate
in the body, in community, and in the earth
that they cannot confine. The difference
is in love; the difference is in grief and joy.
Remember the body's pleasure and its sorrow.
Remember its grief at the loss of all it knew.
Remember its redemption in suffering
and in love. Remember its resurrection
on the last day, when all made things
that have not refused this passage
will return, clarified, each fully being
in the being of all. Remember the small
secret creases of the earth—the grassy,
the wooded, and the rocky—that the water
has made, finding its way. Remember
the voices of the water flowing. Remember
the water flowing under the shadows
of the trees, of the tall grasses, of the stone.
Remember the water striders walking over
the surface of the water as it flowed.
Remember the great sphere of the small
wren's song, through which the water flowed
and the light fell. Remember, and come to rest
in light's ordinary miracle.

Wendell Berry

Plasma

The cathedral has fossils
of sea-creatures in its wells,
these stones
have been under water,
unimagined fish
have swum through this skin.

I stand in a shell of rock
holding my ear
to echoes from long-dead oceans,
waves trapped
in acanthus leaves,
seabeds carved in a rose window.

Marble in floor and arcade
have come from earth's core,
steps hewn from the sun,
pillars and buttresses
sprung out of supernovas.

Moon and stars have bloomed
into people and church
which claims the final alchemy.
God meeting us
in the radiations of prayer.
Love unsettling dust.

Isobel Thrilling

Self-Portrait

It doesn't interest me if there is one God
or many gods.
I want to know if you belong or feel
abandoned.
If you know despair or can see it in others.
I want to know
if you are prepared to live in the world
with its harsh need
to change you. If you can look back
with firm eyes
saying this is where I stand. I want to know
if you know
how to melt into that fierce heat of living
falling toward
the centre of your longing. I want to know
if you are willing
to live, day by day, with the consequence of love
and the bitter
unwanted passion of your sure defeat.

I have heard, in *that* fierce embrace, even
the gods speak of God.

David Whyte

Confessional

I come once more to this terrible place;
As it was it is, each stone and each face

Unchanged, making an index of the change
In me. Everything here was arranged

Long ago; the wind, raking from the north,
Saw to that. I hear it now. In the hearth

Coals glow and the ash flies early and late;
Every face is ruckled, sands corrugate;

Inland, those superstitious hawthorn trees
Strain away from the wind and heckled seas.

Yet I come. Here alone I cannot sham.
The place insists that I know who I am.

Elemental trinity—earth, air, sea—
Harshly advocate my humility:

You are bigoted, over-ambitious,
You are proud, you salute the meretricious.

Then I have altered this much with the years:
That I need more to admit my errors,

From fear, and a longing not to be blind;
So I am scoured by the unchanging wind,

And rid again of some superfluity
By that force uninterested in me.

And I can go, prepared for the possible;
Dream and bone set out from the confessional.

Kevin Crossley-Holland

Mantra

Everything turns away,
All things arise and fall—
The buzzard turning the hill
Through the jewelled mill of his eye,
The seashell turned to stone
In the slow tides of shale,
The larch lost in cloud,
The shepherd's call on the air.
The pirouetting hare
Patrols the high wood,
Rain polishes rock,
The stone bridge swallows the stream:
Nothing is still the same.
Where is stillness found?
All things arise and turn,
Everything falls away.

Grevel Lindop

Jinja

Though the boys selling Coke at Jinja,
the source of the Nile, have never heard of Egypt,
kingfishers know to point their bills like telescopic
sights and dive; emerge with silver in their beaks,
and the perfume of the Nile in their feathers.

At the river's edge, above the stagnant pool,
red dragonflies advertise their passion;
ignore the disappointment of water
burned to dust at the margins,
never to flow on the great journey.

Flies bright as rubies
move in binary waves
across the river's silver plains:
moving to the rhythms of their race,
if they pierce the river's veil, they drown.

What watches me, beyond the veil?
What watches all the rivers
gliding through my heart?
At the end of my journey,
what sea, what planet waits for me?

In the kayak of my mind I set off
with the faith of horizons, not knowing
what rapids or falls of fire I face, or what
canyons and chasms, what echoes
in what dried-out beds await.

Yet I hear only the rivers and seas turning their wheel;
sense this is no time to question the wisdom
of water, nor the source of all that flows.
I only know these eyes, the sudden dive—
the joy of flight with silver in my beak.

Philip Wells

The Boy in the Bell

Over my head the balance of Nature
Is like looking into the future

The honeysuckle the blackberry
They laugh at history

And the cobweb is the secret score
To the music we are searching for.

Hugo Williams

A California Requiem

I walked among the equidistant graves
New planted in the irrigated lawn.
The square, trim headstones quietly declared
The impotence of grief against the sun.

There were no outward signs of human loss.
No granite angel wept beside the lane.
No bending willow broke the once-rough ground
Now graded to a geometric plane.

My blessed California, you are so wise,
You render death abstract, efficient, clean.
Your afterlife is only real estate,
And in his kingdom Death must stay unseen.

I would have left then. I had made my one
Obligatory visit to the dead.
But as I turned to go, I heard the voices,
Faint but insistent. This is what they said.

"Stay a moment longer, quiet stranger.
Your footsteps woke us from our lidded cells.
Now hear us whisper in the scorching wind,
Our single voice drawn from a thousand hells.

"We lived in places that we never knew.
We could not name the birds perched on our sill,
Or see the trees we cut down for our view.
What we possessed we always chose to kill.

"We claimed the earth but did not hear her claim,
And when we died, they laid us on her breast,
But she refuses us — until we earn
Forgiveness from the lives we dispossessed.

"We are so tiny now — light as the spores
That rotting clover sheds into the air,
Dry as old pods burnt open by the sun,
Barren as seeds unrooted anywhere.

"Forget your stylish verses, little poet —
So sadly beautiful, precise, and tame.

We are your people, though you would deny it.
Admit the justice of our primal claim.

"Become the voice of our forgotten places.
Teach us the names of what we have destroyed.
We are like shadows the bright noon erases,
Weightlessly shrinking, bleached into the void.

"We offer you the landscape of your birth—
Exquisite and despoiled. We all share blame.
We cannot ask forgiveness of the earth
For killing what we cannot even name."

Dana Gioia

The Andean Flute

He dances to that music in the wood
As if history were no more than a dream.
Who said the banished gods were gone for good?

The furious rhythm creates a manic mood,
Piercing the twilight like a mountain stream.
He dances to that music in the wood.

We might have put on Bach or Buxtehude,
But a chance impulse chose the primal scream.
Who said the banished gods were gone for good?

An Inca frenzy fires his northern blood.
He child-heart picking up the tribal beam,
He dances to that music in the wood.

A puff of snow bursts where the birches brood;
Along the lane the earliest snowdrops gleam.
Who said the banished gods were gone for good?

It is the ancient cry for warmth and food
That moves him. Acting out an ancient theme,
He dances to that music in the wood.
Who said the banished gods were gone for good?

Derek Mahon

The Pool

I will always smile at my neighbour.
And I will always speak to God alone,
Beside the hidden pool.

Why is it that by that pool
No two humans can speak—not even lovers—
Without the dark falling and the Gods
Shutting their delicate hearts like clams?

All we can do is bide our time by the pool,
Listen in air clear as springwater

And gently carry the hush back—
Cupped in our hands.

Philip Wells

Soil

What colour would you call that now? That brown
which is not precisely the colour of excrement
or suede?
The depth has you hooked. Has it a scent
of its own, a peculiar adhesiveness? Is it weighted,
borne down

by its own weight? It creeps under your skin
like a landscape that's a mood, or a thought
in mid-birth,
and suddenly a dull music has begun. You're caught
by your heels in that grudging lyrical earth,
a violin

scraped and scratched, and there is nowhere to go
but home, which is nowhere to be found
and yet
is here, unlost, solid, the very ground
on which you stand but cannot visit
or know.

George Szirtes

The Dawn Chorus

It is not sleep itself but dreams we miss,
Say the psychologists; and the poets too.
We yearn for that reality in this.

There is another world resides in this,
Said Éluard — not original, but true.
It is not sleep itself but dreams we miss.

If we could once achieve a synthesis
Of the archaic and the entirely new . . .
We yearn for that reality in this.

But, wide awake, clear-eyed with cowardice,
The flaming seraphim we find untrue.
It is not sleep itself but dreams we miss.

Listening heart-broken to the dawn chorus,
Clutching the certainty that once we flew,
We yearn for that reality in this.

Awaiting still our metamorphosis,
We hoard the fragments of what once we knew.
It is not sleep itself but dreams we miss.
We yearn for that reality in this.

Derek Mahon

A. M.

for Lee Rust Brown

. . . And here the dark infinitive to feel,
Which would endure and have the earth be still
And the star-strewn night pour down the mountains
Into the hissing fields and silent towns until the last
Insomniac turned in, must end, and early risers see
The scarlet clouds break up and golden plumes of smoke
From uniform dark homes turn white, and so on down
To the smallest blade of grass and fallen leaf
Touched by the arriving light. Another day has come,
Another fabulous escape from the damages of night,
So even the gulls, in the ragged circle of their flight,
Above the sea's long lanes that flash and fall, scream
Their approval. How well the sun's rays probe
The rotting carcass of a skate, how well
They show the worms and swarming flies at work,
How well they shine upon the fatal sprawl
Of everything on earth. How well they love us all.

Mark Strand

The End

Not every man knows what he shall sing at the end,
Watching the pier as the ship sails away, or what it will seem like
When he's held by the sea's roar, motionless, there at the end,
Or what he shall hope for once it is clear that he'll never go back.

When the time has passed to prune the rose or caress the cat,
When the sunset torching the lawn and the full moon icing it down
No longer appear, not every man knows what he'll discover instead.
When the weight of the past leans against nothing, and the sky

Is no more than remembered light, and the stories of cirrus
And cumulus come to a close, and all the birds are suspended in flight,
Not every man knows what is waiting for him, or what he shall sing
When the ship he is on slips into darkness, there at the end.

Mark Strand

Ordination

From the scuttlings of a hundred and seventy lives
we pressed in. We brimmed the chapel, on graves

stood tip-toe, to witness, all at once, what *we* do
sniffing by inches, by crisis, by illness; to hear you

vow, carve your name in a marble groove, dare
break from cover, stand in the cross-hairs,

announce to Fate your fate, bait chance,
shake your fist at the snake-eyed dice.

You put on God like a coat of holes, drink in God
like bullets; start where the Dead go.

A mouse in the peregrine claw grows wings, grows wide
over his old field.

Martin Schmandt

The Poet Answers the Accuser

No matter what I am,
For if I tell of winter lightning, stars and hail,
Of white waves, pale Hebridean sun,
It is not I who see, who hear, who tell, but all
Those cloud-born drops the scattering wind has blown
To be regathered in the stream of ocean,
The many in the one;
For these I am,
Water, wind and stone I am,
Grey birds that ride the storm and the cold waves I am,
And what can my words say,
Who am a drop in ocean's spray,
A bubble of white foam,
Who am a breath of wandering air,
But what the elements in me cry
That in my making take their joy,
In my unmaking go their way?
I am, but do not know, my song,
Nor to what scale my sense is tuned
Whose music trembles through me and flows on.
A note struck by the stars I am,
A memory-trace of sun and moon and moving waters,
A voice of the unnumbered dead, fleeting as they —
What matter who I am?

Kathleen Raine

As for Poets

As for poets
The Earth Poets
Who write small poems,
Need help from no man.

The Air Poets
Play out the swiftest gales
And sometimes loll in the eddies.
Poem after poem,
Curling back on the same thrust.

At fifty below
Fuel oil won't flow
And propane stays in the tank.
Fire Poets
Burn at absolute zero
Fossil love pumped back up.

The first
Water Poet
Stayed down six years.
He was covered with seaweed.
The life in his poem
Left million of tiny
Different tracks
Criss-crossing through the mud.

With the Sun and Moon
In his belly,
The Space Poet
Sleeps.
No end to the sky —
But his poems,
Like wild geese,
Fly off the edge.

A Mind Poet
Stays in the house.
The house is empty
And it has no walls.
The poem
Is seen from all sides,
Everywhere,
At once.

Gary Snyder

A Vision

If we will have the wisdom to survive,
to stand like slow growing trees
on a ruined place, renewing, enriching it,
if we will make our season welcome here,
asking not too much of earth or heaven,
then a long time after we are dead
the lives our lives prepare will live
here, their houses strongly placed
along the valley sides, fields and gardens
rich in the windrows. *The river will run
clear*, as we will never know it,
and over it, birdsong like a canopy.
On the levels of the hills will be
green meadows, stock bells in noon shade.
On the steeps where greed and ignorance cut down
the old forest, *an old forest will stand*,
its rich leaf-fall drifting on its roots.
The veins of forgotten springs will have opened.
Families will be singing in the fields.
In their voices they will hear a music
risen out of the ground. They will take
nothing from the ground they will not return,
whatever the grief at parting. Memory,
native to this valley, will spread over it
like a grove, and *memory will grow
into legend, legend into song, song
into sacrament*. The abundance of this place,
the songs of its people and its birds,
will be health and wisdom and indwelling
light. This is no paradisal dream.
Its hardship is its possibility.

Wendell Berry

What It Is

It is
whatever it is
that stirs the house

of your heart,
that shares
your hunger,

your thirst,
your urge all day
to hear more

than your own voice
voicing its foolishness.

It is
whatever it is
in your hands

that slithers away,
whoever can only be
glimpsed, sudden

or sharp, but tuneless,
bass notes, not
melody.

You were born
knowing

you'd have to learn
whoever it would take
and even to learn

what to make of it.
It is not
the words

in your throat
not even
your honest intention.

When you open
your mouth

it is
whatever it is
that no longer speaks

that longs to speak,
whatever it is
that trembles.

Andrea Hollander Budy

For the Dancers
for Miodrag Pavlović

I
Cut twigs of green willow and plait a wreath
And lean it against a stone on the heath

Trim sprigs of green willow and weave a crown
One for each child   who was cut down

Plant stakes of green willow and fix a ring
One for each child who was felled   for nothing

Bring pitchforks and shovels and mallets and staves
Hang rings of green willow over their graves

> *Dance   gypsy butterfly*
> *On the air between earth and sky*
> *Dance for the Green Rider*

II
Cut a pine branch and prune a rod
Beat out the demons and call up God

Strip an ash-bough and peel a wand
Whip out our ghosts to back-of-beyond

Find a hazel-fork   dowse for a well
Flush out the dead and clean out Hell

Trim a willow-switch   carve a cane
Spur hope to pulse and race again

>   *Dance   gypsy butterfly*
>   *On the air between earth and sky*
>   *Dance for the Green Rider*

III
Past sedimented fires and bones
Past scattered cairns and standing stones

Past skulls immured in bloodied walls
Crushed corridors and unroofed halls

Past desecrated monasteries
And all the vanquished histories

Of libraries gone up in smoke
Volumes ancestors wrote or spoke

>   *Dance   gypsy butterfly*
>   *On the air between earth and sky*
>   *Dance for the Green Rider*

IV
Past ancient mounts and pits and caves
Past fresh sites of unmarked graves

Past dandelion and celandine
Take a sprig tipped with the cone of a pine

Bound round with basil and fennel and sorrel
And what if the laws of our bitter blood quarrel

Demand more revenge and bitter blood feud
Deny them   and dance for the day that's renewed

> *Dance   gypsy butterfly*
> *On the air between earth and sky*
> *Dance for the Green Rider*

V
Dance on   though whips of lightning crack
On the hill's flank   on the wood's back

And gongs of thunder boom and toll
And louring stormclouds clash and roll

Then once the chords of the rain have thinned
Into random notes   and the wail of the wind

Has dropped   a half-heard delicate thrumming
Will whisper   The time for new dance is coming

> *Dance   gypsy butterfly*
> *On the air between earth and sky*
> *Dance for the Green Rider*

VI
In glades where wild hawthorn has spilt
Its blossom-dappled springtime quilt

And hyacinth and violet
Mark patterns on a moving net

Of colour flecked with depths of shade
As if light touched there   a world remade

Come   beat your breasts   you dervishes
And purge us of our anguishes

> *Dance   gypsy butterfly*
> *On the air between earth and sky*
> *Dance for the Green Rider*

VIII

Between these hills and our roofed home
Between these clouds and the starry dome

Between the bride and the bridegroom
Between the nursery-cot and tomb

Gaudy gypsy   write light on air
Brush out our sorrow and all despair

And draw peace in   and help it hold
With showers for silver and sun for gold

> *Dance   gypsy butterfly*
> *On the air between earth and sky*
> *Dance for the Green Rider*

Richard Burns

Do we become

In the threshing of the crop and the thrashing of a tree,
at the midnight hour, in a midflight soar,
water striking stone, wind turning vane,
the racing of the wave, the chasing of the shade,
the mystery of wine, the breaking of time,
stalk cut, blood let, up root,
owl hoot, lamb bleat, night jar,
breeze through a door, light dance on the floor,
cloth shaken, folded, lain in a drawer,
wool wound, tower round, bell sound,
leap, lilt, low, lope,
echo, thunder, clatter, glance,
rattle, tumble, tremble, chance,
clouds build, count yield, wound healed:
not in the pull and push of passion's plea
do we become, but in this downdive into self
for each coin, every piece, of this world's wealth.

Frances Howarth

Prayer

Here I work in the hollow of God's hand
with Time bent round into my reach. I touch
the circle of the earth, I throw and catch
the sun and moon by turns into my mind.
I sense the length of it from end to end,
I sway me gently in my flesh and each
point of the process changes as I watch;
the flowers come, the rain follows the wind.

And all I ask is this—and you can see
how far the soul, when it goes under flesh,
is not a soul, is small and creaturish—
that every day the sun comes silently
to set my hands to work and that the moon
turns and returns to meet me when it's done.

Alice Oswald

Midsummer Prayer

In midsummer, under the luminous
sky of everlasting light,

the laced structures of thought
fall away

like the filigrees of the white
diaphanous

dandelion turned pure white and
ghostly,

hovering at the edge of its own
insubstantial

discovery in flight. I'll do the same,
watch

the shimmering dispersal of tented
seeds

lodge in the tangled landscape
without

the least discrimination. So let my own
hopes

escape the burning wreck of ambition,
parachute

through the hushed air, let them spread
elsewhere,

into the tangled part of life that refuses
to be set straight.

Herod searched for days looking for
the children.

The mind's hunger for fame will hunt down
all innocence.

Let them find safety in the growing wild.
I'll not touch them there.

David Whyte

Night

Do not wake me, for I am not ready
to speak, to break the spell
fixed in these sleeping stones.

Go quietly here. Whisper to wise men
what you cannot speak aloud.
Quiet the metal of doors.

It is the time of earth-changes,
of vanishing rainfall,
and the restless barking of dogs.

Divided is the man of hidden
purpose, and evil his redemption.

Harness the wind and drive the water,
you that govern,
who yoke and stride the world . . .

And then be still.

Leaves of the one standing tree
fall through the twilight;
the nightborn images rise, the owl

in the mask of the dreamer wakes:
Who is the guest?
Who is it who knocks and whispers?

As one calmed in his death-dream
would never return
to this hunted world —

one more key to the clockwork
that drives the sunned machine,
another cry under the wheel . . .

But calmed and stationed aloft,
delight in his distance,
to see on the star-pavilions

the bright, imperial creatures rise,
ascend their thrones, rule
and prosper. The thrones darken,

earth in the moon-shadow fails,
and he alone in that cold
and drifting waste keeps alight

memorial constellations . . .

So I in this quiet sleep of stone
can say to you: Leave to me
this one sustaining solace—

my night that has more night
to come. To the sun that has set,
whose dawn I cannot see . . .

Mute in my transformation,
and do not wake me.

John Haines

Offering

Opening I give

thanks, Mother
I give it

for the joy
      in the flickering

for the opening

the gold salmon and green
the vibrating water
      for the floating
I give it

for the star
the face turning under

for the doorways
for the passion
I leap
       to the hill
the warmth

I leap to the gong
of earth

for the drummers
the celebrants, Mother
I give it
       I leap it
strewing flowers

I open, Mother
in the warm
dark of the doorway
I thrum

dissolve

in both hands
Mother

I give it

Carolyn Finlay

For the Children

The rising hills, the slopes,
of statistics
lie before us.
the steep climb
of everything, going up,
up, as we all
go down.

In the next century
or the one beyond that,
they say,
are valleys, pastures,
we can meet there in peace
if we make it.

To climb these coming crests
one word to you, to
you and your children:

stay together
learn the flowers
go light

Gary Snyder

A-Z List of Poets and their Poems
with Sources and Acknowledgements

Every effort has been made to contact all copyright holders. Green Books will be pleased to rectify at the earliest opportunity any omissions or errors brought to their notice.

Abbs, Peter
'The Storm Cloud', 'Road-Side Deaths', 'At Cuckmere Estuary', 'Song of Orpheus', 'Ars Poetica' from *Selected Poems* published by Halfacrown Press. Copyright © Peter Abbs.

Abbot, Josephine
'Canute' published in *Acumen*. Copyright © Josephine Abbot.

Atkinson, Donald
'Chrysanths' and 'Orpheus Attending' from *Graffiti for Hard Hearts* published by Arc Publications. Copyright © Donald Atkinson.

Barker, Sebastian
'The Green Aphis' and 'The Thin End of the Wedge'. Copyright © Sebastian Barker.

Berry, Wendell
'Sabbaths', 'A Vision' first published in *Resurgence*. Copyright © Wendell Berry.

Bhatt, Sujata
'Point No Point' from *Point No Point* published by Carcanet Press. Copyright © Sujata Bhatt.

Bolam, Robyn
'Topsoil, 'Magnolia Tree' from *The Peepshow Girl* published by Bloodaxe Books. 'Between Voyages' from *Raiding the Borders* published by Bloodaxe Books. Both published under the name of Marion Lomax. Copyright © Robyn Bolam.

Boland, Eavan
'A Sparrow-Hawk in the Suburbs', 'Moths', 'This Moment' from *In a Time of Violence* published by Bloodaxe Books. Copyright © Eavan Boland.

Minhinnick, Robert
'Dragonfly', 'Sap', 'Driving in Fog', 'Grandfather in the Garden' from *Selected Poems* published by Carcanet Press. Copyright © Robert Minhinnick.

O'Reilly, Catrióne
'A Brief History of Light', 'On a Dropped Feather', 'Augury', 'Sleep and Spiders' from *The Nowhere Birds* published by Bloodaxe Books. Copyright © Catrióne O'Reilly.

Oswald, Alice
'April', 'The Apple Shed', 'Pruning in Frost', 'Prayer' from *The Thing in the Gap-Stone Wall* published by Oxford University Press. Copyright © Alice Oswald.

Pierpoint, Katherine
'The Twist in the River' from *Truffle Beds* published by Faber & Faber. Copyright © Katherine Pierpoint.

Poole, Richard
'Air: an Aria', 'The Objective Naturalist', 'Below Cym Bychan' from *Natural Histories* published by University of Wales Press. Copyright © Richard Poole.

Poster, Jem
'Plenty', 'Back', 'Archangel', 'Appletree' from *Brought to Light* published by Bloodaxe Books. Copyright © Jem Poster.

Poulson, Joan
'Love-song' from *onetreesinging* published by Blackthorn Books. Copyright © Joan Poulson.

Powell, Neil
'Wood Farm' from *At The Edge* published by Carcanet Press. Copyright © Neil Powell.

Raine, Kathleen
'Amo Ergo Sum', 'Turner's Seas', 'The Poet Answers the Accusers' from *Collected Poems* published by Golgonooza Press. Copyright © Kathleen Raine.

Ramsay, Jay
'Beginning' from *In the Valley of Shadow* published by Diamond Press. 'Homage to Celan'. Copyright © Jay Ramsay.

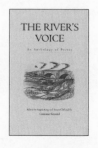

ONLY CONNECT
The Best of Resurgence 1990-1999
edited by John Lane and Maya Kumar Mitchell

This selection of thirty-six articles from *Resurgence* magazine commemorates the publication of the journal's 200th edition, and also twenty-five years of the editorship of Satish Kumar and June Mitchell.

So, what is Resurgence? It is a journal of considerable breadth—a breadth stemming from insights into the tides and reflexes of our global condition to the abiding riches of those with the courage to create and dream. Amongst its themes is the fundamental destructiveness of the global economy; the need for an economics 'as if people mattered'; the importance of size, rurality, non-violence and the Third World. In May 1966 when the first issue was published, most of these issues were 'beyond the pale' of acceptable dinner conversation; today they are becoming even trendy! Resurgence's aim is to mount a sustained attack on the dominant paradigm, yet provocative as it can certainly be, it is never negative, never merely analytical, never merely learned. It is always happy with the wisdom of beauty, the value of practical example and, no less, the importance of the whole, the holistic view of life. 'Only connect', wrote E. M. Forster; it might preface every edition. *288pp 234 x 156mm ISBN 1 870098 90 0 £12.95 pb*

AT HOME ON THE EARTH

A New Selection of the Later Writings of Richard Jefferies
selected and introduced by Jeremy Hooker

Richard Jefferies (1848-87) has long been recognized as an interpreter of English country life and a natural observer with few if any equals. He was an idealist, who believed that human beings could free themselves from outworn ideas and achieve a greatly enlarged spiritual and physical capacity. A 'poet-naturalist' with an ecological vision, who understood the place of human beings in relation to the 'household' of life on earth, he was both mystic and realist, and his writings show the beauty of 'wild England' but also the harsh conditions of labouring life in the Victorian countryside. Jeremy Hooker's new selection represents Jefferies at his best, and reveals his contemporary significance. *176 pp 234 x 156mm ISBN 1 903998 02 6 £9.95 pb*

www.greenbooks.co.uk

Resurgence

Resurgence magazine has been described in *The Guardian* as "the spiritual and artistic flagship of the green movement". If you would like a sample copy of a recent issue, please contact:

Jeanette Gill
Rocksea Farmhouse,
St. Mabyn, Bodmin
Cornwall PL30 3BR
Telephone & fax 01208 841824
www.resurgence.org